Co-Piloting™

A Handbook for Mentors of Children

By Robert P. Bowman, Ph.D. and Susan C. Bowman, Ed.S., LPC

**Effective Skills and Strategies
for Reaching and Encouraging
Elementary School Youth**

© 1997 by
YouthLight, Inc.
Chapin, SC 29036

Illustrations by Walt Lardner
Cover Illustration by Sandra Shelton
Layout & Design by Andover Graphics and Elizabeth Madden
Project Editing by Rebecca VanGilder

ISBN 1-889636-04-5

10 9 8 7 6 5 4 3 2
Printed in the United States of America

Dedication

To our three daughters April, Melissa, and Autumn, and grandson Calvin, whom we hope will become mentors themselves, someday.

Acknowledgments

We would like to thank the following people for their contributions to our books:

Rebecca VanGilder, Lisa Nordlund and Melissa White proofread the manuscripts and contributed to the readability of the books.

The following people provided reviews of the program and provided many valuable suggestions:

- Arlonial Bradford-Jackson
- Josh Lorick
- Lollie Becton
- Norma Colwell
- Ron Miles

Julie Chibarro reviewed the program and provided us with supplemental articles for our review of the literature on mentoring.

We would also like to thank all the professionals we met during seminars and conferences we conducted around the United States during the past nine years. We learned much from the hundreds of people who tried out parts of our mentoring program, and sent us information or told us about their programs.

Lastly, we would like to thank God for being our foremost mentor. Without His guidance and blessings, this work would not have been completed.

Table of Contents

Chapter 1

Building a Foundation

"A hundred years from now it will not matter what my bank account was, the sort of house I lived in, or the kind of car I drove... But the world may be different because I was important in the life of a child."

Author Unknown

Building a Foundation

Most people remember with fondness at least one person who had a special, positive impact on their life. This "influencer" was most likely someone who gave them extra attention and encouragement, and communicated a deep belief in their potential.

Unfortunately, many disadvantaged young people will not find such a positive influencer by chance. This is why the Co-Piloting Mentor Program was developed. This program provides trained mentors (Co-Pilots) for young people (Pilots) who need extra support and encouragement in their lives. These Pilots can be as young as pre-kindergartners and as old as 12th graders.

What is a Co-Pilot?

A Co-Pilot is a volunteer mentor to a needy child. He/she works to provide this child with a special, encouraging relationship that will hopefully become a foundation for success in that child's life. Through this relationship, a Co-Pilot attempts to foster the child's self-worth, success-motivation, coping skills, and character strengths. The Co-Piloting program provides specialized training and other kinds of support to help ensure that this mentoring relationship will be a positive experience for both mentor and child.

Real co-pilots receive <u>specialized</u> training. They learn a particular set of skills and procedures, and develop a clear understanding of their responsibilities. They also learn that they are not ultimately in command of the flight, that's the pilot's job. In addition, they learn how to provide crucial background assistance for the pilot, providing navigation and trouble-shooting if needed.

Similarly, a Co-Pilot mentor learns a specialized set of skills and procedures to become an encourager, navigator, and back-up flyer to his or her pilot (child). Ultimately, a Co-Pilot mentor works to help a disadvantaged child learn how to take flight and soar to new heights in his or her life.

Who Needs a Co-Pilot?

Many disadvantaged children do not have positive role models in
their lives. Instead, they are constantly bombarded by
various media with examples of negative heroes
who they come to idolize. These children also
tend to admire older juveniles who may
"hang out" near their homes, or who
are friends with their older siblings.
Without opportunities to work with
encouraging mentors, these
children are likely to follow the
same negative life styles
they see around them
each day.

For example, some children as young as kindergartners have already developed negative attitudes toward learning and schoolwork. These young people have already started believing that they are incapable of succeeding in school. This negative attitude consumes children's motivation and encourages the beginning of a cycle of failure in school.

Unfortunately, there are many children like this who desperately need increased opportunities to relate with encouraging, attentive adults. Some of these children, for example, have not had the opportunity to live with two parents. Others have lost a parent through divorce, abandonment or death. Still other children have parents who do not spend much time with them. These children are especially vulnerable to negative influences and desperately need more opportunities to experience relationships with positive role models.

There are many problems that affect today's young people. Talking about these difficulties is a favorite pastime among many adults. Congratulations! You have decided to go beyond talking and actually take some action to help one of these young people. By volunteering for this program, you are taking the first step that might eventually turn around a young child's life.

What is the "Right Stuff" That Makes an Effective Co-Pilot?

Becoming an effective Co-Pilot is not an easy task. You may face challenges from time to time. Navigating through turbulent times with your young Pilot will require you to use many of the abilities you already have and the strategies you will learn from this program.

Co-Piloting is not, however, just about working with your child's difficulties. Often the benefits are mutual for you and the child. Relating in a playful, encouraging manner with your child will provide you both with many fun and personally uplifting experiences. Your work with your Pilot will provide you both with many joyful and meaningful experiences.

An effective Co-Pilot is someone who has the skill, ability, and commitment to help bring about positive changes in a needy young person's life. First and foremost, your Pilot must come to see that you possess and display certain personal characteristics. The following activity will help you explore these qualities which are the foundation of effective mentoring.

Activity 1.1: Think of a Mentor

Directions: As you grew up, there were probably several people who had positive influences on your life. However, some of these people influenced you more than others.

Think of a positive mentor you once had. Perhaps it was someone older than you whom you admired and tried to emulate. On the lines below, write some of the positive qualities that this person exhibited.

Teachers _____

HS Guidence Con. _____

BB couch _____

Co-Pilot Characteristics

There are many qualities that distinguish mentors from other people who are less effective influencers. Look through the following seven qualities and compare them to your list. If you have time, discuss each of these characteristics with other Co-Pilots.

Caring

A Co-Pilot has a deep regard for the value and dignity of the Pilot.

Outgoing

A Co-Pilot is friendly, fun loving, and approachable.

Persistent

A Co-Pilot is committed to persevere during rough times.

Insightful

A Co-Pilot is sensitive to the Pilot's cultural, gender, and religious perspectives.

Link

A Co-Pilot connects the Pilot with outside resources when needed.

Open-Minded

A Co-Pilot shows acceptance of the Pilot's worth and potential, regardless of his or her past actions.

Trustworthy

A Co-Pilot shows that he/she is dependable and genuine.

Co-Piloting Roles

To be effective with your Pilot, you will need to continually demonstrate these "Co-Pilot Characteristics." The following are ways that you can show these characteristics to your Pilot.

The Co-Pilot should be seen by the Pilot as a(n):

Good Listener who will be there when needed.

Fun Person who is playful.

Tutor who will help with schoolwork.

Teacher who will encourage learning.

Coach who will help build skills and confidence.

Guide who helps with setting and achieving goals.

Encourager who motivates others.

Role Model who is admired and should be emulated.

Through your dedication to assuming these roles, your young Pilot will benefit in many ways. Your special support and encouragement will help your Pilot develop feelings of self-worth and self-confidence.

Activity 1.2: Ground Rules for Co-Pilots

Directions: Pair up with another Co-Pilot, or join with a small group of participants. Then, discuss one of the ground rules from the following list. In particular, talk about the importance of the rule and what each Co-Pilot should do to ensure that the rule will be followed. When finished, have a representative of your group present a summary of their discussion to the other Co-Pilots.

1. **Confidentiality:** Even with the youngest Pilot, keep specific information that he/she tells you in confidence unless:
   a. Your Pilot has given you permission, or
   b. There is evidence of danger to your Pilot or others. Then, you must tell the Program Coordinator and/or someone to whom you have been directed to refer such cases.

2. **Charity:** Do not become a "Santa Claus" to your Pilot. Too much emphasis on material gifts will work against the development of a healthy mentoring relationship. It is okay, however, to purchase some inexpensive items for your Pilot like incentives, greeting cards, small gifts, or a portfolio cover.

3. **School Policy:** If you are planning to meet your Pilot at school, you must be aware of and follow any school policies that might apply to your work with a student.

4. **Outside Meetings:** If you are planning to meet with your Pilot anywhere other than the school setting, you must first make your Program Coordinator aware and acquire parental/guardian permission.

5. **Commitments:** You must keep your commitments to your Pilot. Too many missed appointments can lead to initial feelings of discouragement and eventually lead to feelings of abandonment in a young person.

6. **Support Group Meetings:** You must attend your Co-Pilot Support Group Meetings. These meetings will provide you and other Co-Pilots with opportunities to share ideas and concerns with each other.

7. **Role Modeling:** Each time you meet with your Pilot, remember to show the seven Co-Pilot Characteristics described earlier in this chapter.

8. **Self-Preservation:** Make sure you take care of yourself and have many fun times with your Pilot!

Activity 1.3: Three Co-Piloting Stories

Directions: In the Appendix on pages 124- 129, three people tell of their experiences as Co-Pilots. Reading and comparing these stories will help you develop a more personalized understanding of what some other Co-Pilots have experienced in their programs.

Note that each of the three stories is told by a Co-Pilot from a different kind of program. In "Martha's Story" the Co-Pilot is a teacher. In "William's Story" the Co-Pilot is a corporate employee. In "Shane's Story" the Co-Pilot is a college student.

Discussion Questions:

After reading all three Co-Piloting stories, discuss your answers to each of the following questions.

1. What experiences did the three Co-Pilots have that were most similar to each other?

2. What approaches did the Co-Pilots feel were the most effective in helping their Pilots? *Talking to her alot and getting her mother for a little help.*

3. What do you believe is the most important role a Co-Pilot can play for a young person? *a best friend. and the other help young person by getting a tutor.*

Chapter 2

Relationship-Building Tactics

*"Real unselfishness consists in sharing
the interests of others."*
George Santayana

Relationship-Building Tactics

As a Co-Pilot, you should not think of mentoring as merely looking for your young person's problems and then working to resolve them. The single most important thing that you can do for your Pilot is to provide him/her with a special, positive kind of relationship that will be remembered for a lifetime.

This special relationship will help your child discover many positive things about him/herself. During your meetings, as you provide recurring attention and encouragement, your child will begin to build on his or her self-worth and confidence.

However, realistically there is no guarantee that a close Pilot/Co-Pilot relationship will develop between you and your child. Even if you seem to "hit it off" with your Pilot at the beginning, you may later face challenges in your relationship. Sometimes you may need to be very patient and use every encouraging skill that you can think of. In time, your Pilot will learn to become more comfortable with you and to trust in your helping efforts.

In the previous chapter, we covered the characteristics of an effective Co-Pilot. Now, let's look at the keys to using these characteristics to build an encouraging relationship with your Pilot.

Four Keys to Start a Mentoring Relationship

1. Listen Attentively
2. Ask Inviting Questions
3. Summarize Content and Feeling
4. Use Strategic Self-Disclosures

1. Listen Attentively

One of the greatest gifts someone can give to a young person is to patiently listen in a deeply caring manner. We may seek out a good listener for ourselves when we have experiences we want to share. Unfortunately, good listeners are difficult to find in today's fast-paced world. Some people don't even take time to carefully and patiently listen to the feelings of their own family members.

Young people become excited when someone encourages them to talk about their interests, concerns, and views of events. For children to develop positive beliefs about their self-worth, they need for someone to show a special interest in them. This means having a person in their lives who will take the time periodically to be an encouraging listener.

As you begin your relationship with your Pilot, you should work especially hard to be a good listener. Attentive listening begins by displaying open and inviting body language to the child. As your Pilot talks, or plays:

Don't cross your arms, lean too far back, fidget with something in your hands, or look away very often from your Pilot's face.

Do sit with an open, calm posture, perhaps on the floor or in a low chair, directly facing the child. Laugh with him/her and keep a facial expression that shows genuine interest in what he/she is saying or doing.

Activity 2.1: Inviting and Uninviting Body Language

Directions: Pair up with another participant and decide who will be the first "Talker." The other person will be the "Listener."

Sit directly facing one another. The Talker should begin by telling about something that happened to him/her during the past month.

At first, the Listener should display positive or "inviting" body language to show he/she is listening attentively. After about 15 seconds, the Listener should start to appear increasingly distracted by:

- Crossing his or her arms and leaning back.
- Looking away from the Talker's face, perhaps staring at his or her watch, then glancing at others in the room.
- Stretching and yawning.
- Using other creative ideas to show as much distraction as possible.

After two minutes, stop and discuss what happened. Then, start the activity again, but this time the same Listener should try to show the Co-Piloting Characteristics through inviting body language. Use the same topic and allow enough time for the Talker to finish his or her story.

Once you and your partner have each had a turn being inviting and uninviting listeners, discuss your answers to the following questions.

Discussion Questions:

1. As a talker, what was it like trying to tell your story to such an uninviting listener? How did this differ when the person became an inviting listener?

2. What are some common mistakes adults make when listening to children?

3. How can you "listen" to your Pilot if he/she is not talkative?

2. Ask Inviting Questions

Asking children questions can invite them to realize that you are interested in learning more about them and what they are doing. However, some ways of asking questions are clearly better than others. When working with your young Pilot, remember the following hints:

Limit Your Number of Questions: Too many questions can cause a child to feel uncomfortable. He/she may begin to wonder why you want to know so much and what you will be doing with the information.

Avoid "Why" Questions: Questions that begin with "Why" can arouse a child's defenses because it may sound like you are making an accusation. For example, "Why do you feel that way?" is risky to ask a child. A better way to ask this question would be, "What happened that bothered you so much?"

Use "What" or "How" Questions: The most inviting questions for children usually begin with the words, "What" or "How." Though there are many other ways to construct questions, these are usually the most inviting.

The following are examples of inviting "What" and "How" questions for children:

- What is your favorite animal?
- How is that animal like you?
- What is your favorite thing to do in school?
- How would you change school, if you could?
- What do you look for in a friend?
- How can a teacher be helpful to you?
- What do you like to do with your friends?
- How do you make a new friend?

Activity 2.2: Reword the Questions

Directions: Read each of these questions. Then in the space that follows, reword the question using a more inviting "What" or "How" question.

1. Why don't you like school?

   what do you like about school?

2. Are you going to do better next time?

   what can we do to do better next time?

3. Did you work things out with Stephen?

   what is wrong with you and Stephen?

4. Can you tell me about it?

   what happen?

5. Why do you feel that way?

   what made you feel that way?

Follow-Up:
Have one person in your Co-Pilot group tell a brief description of something that happened to him/her during the past week. When the story is finished, brainstorm several possible "What" and "How" questions that could be asked. Be sure that the questions follow the story and do not lead the person away from what was said. Remember, a good question follows the talker's lead and demonstrates that you are interested in what he/she is saying.

3. Summarize Content and Feeling

An even more intensive tactic that will help strengthen your relationship with your Pilot is summarizing content and feeling. That is, when your Pilot talks or plays out something in front of you, occasionally say something that summarizes what the child said or did.

Becoming comfortable with this kind of statement may take some practice if you have never learned it before. When done accurately and in a caring manner, a summary statement can be very powerful. It sends the message that you are interested in the child and want him/her to continue talking.

Summarizing Content

To summarize content, simply listen to and watch your Pilot for awhile. Then periodically make brief statements (not questions) that tell the essence of what he/she is saying or showing. That is, simply tell the child what he/she has just said or done.

Examples

Situation 1: After you ask how he/she is doing, the Pilot says nothing and stares at a box full of toys.

Content Summary: "I see that you notice that box of toys."

Situation 2: Your Pilot tells you about several different things he/she did over the weekend, such as go to a movie, fight with a brother, and go to an uncle's house.

Content Summary: "You did a lot of things last weekend. Let's see. . . you went to see a movie and also went to your uncle's house. You also got into a fight with your brother."

Summarizing Feelings

Sometimes your Pilot will tell or show you some of his/her feelings. These emotions may be primarily pleasant, unpleasant, or both. Whenever you notice an emotion in your Pilot, try to identify a word that seems to best describe that feeling. Then, add this feeling word to your summarization of content. Note that if you hear both pleasant and unpleasant emotions, you may need to include more than one feeling word in your statement.

Don't worry too much about sounding like an "echo chamber" when you tell your Pilot a summary of what he/she said. Children enjoy it when someone repeats back the key points that they are saying. This shows them you care and are very interested in how they feel about things.

Happy   **Excited**   **Calm**

Angry   **Sad**   **Scared**

Examples

Situation 1: A child shows a big smile and laughs with delight as he/she tells you about a birthday party planned for next week.

Feeling Summary: "You are so excited about your birthday party next week!"

Situation 2: A child talks with you about how he/she "hates" everything about school except for recess which is fun.

Feeling Summary: "You are very upset about school, but you do like recess."

Situation 3: A child is smiling while he/she is drawing a picture for you of a boy with arms stretched, flying through the air.

Feeling Summary: "You look like you are having fun drawing the boy flying through the air."

> *Hint: In addition to making these kinds of statements, try to show with your face and voice that you understand and care about the feelings you sense your Pilot is experiencing.*

Activity 2.3:   Constructing Summaries

Directions: For each of the following statements from children, write the best summary you can. Try to include one or more feeling words in each summary.

Kesha: "We got a new puppy last night. And I know it loves me a lot."

wow you got a loving puppy

Timmy: "I like to play computer games. I'm really good at them."

Shweet I love computer games. I am good at them computer games too. Can you bring it in for us to play one day.

Peter: "I hate school! I just can't do anything right."

what don't you like about school. who said you can't anything right. I think you are a great kid and is great at every thing you do with me.

Holly: "Maria has been my best friend for a long time. We like to do lots of things together. But I hate Sarah! She's trying to steal Maria away from me."

aww I am sorry to hear that but here try to be friends with both and have twice as much fun.

Follow-Up:
Similar to the procedures you used in Activity 2.2, have one person in your group tell a brief description of something that happened to him/her during the past year. When the story is finished, brainstorm different ways to summarize content and/or feelings. Be sure that each summarization does not add new information, or end with a question. Rather, a good summarization shows that you are listening carefully and encouraging the talker to continue sharing with you.

4. Use Strategic Self-Disclosures

Self-Disclosure can be a very effective way to communicate to your Pilot that you have some experiences similar to his or her situation. Sometimes, telling your story to your Pilot can be very effective in helping you show that you understand. But, if your story is dragged out or off the topic, it can also backfire and convince the child that you are not very understanding. To be effective, self-disclosures must be brief, relevant, and timely.

As you get to know your child better, it may be helpful to think of one or more stories you can share about yourself that may be similar to his/her experiences. Then, build a strategy of how to share your story briefly, while making it relevant to the child. Next, determine the best time and place to tell it.

Activity 2.4: Building a Plan for Self-Disclosure

Directions: Pair up with another Co-Pilot and exchange handbooks. Then take turns using the following questions to interview each other. Write summaries of your partner's responses in his or her book.

1. What is one of your interests or hobbies?

2. What is one of your greatest personal strengths or characteristics?

3. What is one challenge you had when you were a child?

4. What was one of your greatest accomplishments when you were a child?

Follow-Up:
Look over your responses that your partner wrote in your book. Discuss some good and bad times for sharing this information with a child.

Chapter 3

Take Off and Landing Procedures

"If you fly high or far enough, you'll always find a place where the sun is shining."
Amelia Earhart*

*Amelia Earhart was the first female pilot to fly solo across the Atlantic Ocean. Amelia was lost at sea, presumably in a plane crash, while she was attempting to break another record by flying around the world.

Three Stages of Co-Piloting

Like any mentoring relationship, Co-Piloting has three stages: a beginning stage (Take Off), a middle stage (In Flight), and an ending stage (Landing). Each of these stages involves its own set of challenges and opportunities. Giving careful consideration to the dynamics of each stage will help ensure that you and your Pilot will have a safe and successful journey. This Chapter will emphasize the first and third stages.

Take Off

In the beginning you will want to say and do things to help your relationship get off the ground with your child. Your first meetings together will help you build a foundation that will help strengthen and sustain your relationship over time.

In-Flight

Once the relationship has taken off, you will need to keep the momentum going. For helpful suggestions to use in this phase, refer to Chapters 4 and 5 in this book. In addition, the activities in the "Self-Improvement Lessons" will provide opportunities to help you and your Pilot explore a variety of relevant topics together.

Landing

Preparing for your journey's end with your Pilot takes careful planning. If approached carefully, this transition in your relationship can be meaningful and memorable for both of you.

Take Off

Most children are thrilled to have their own Co-Pilots. They are excited to have someone like you take such a special interest in them. In the beginning, like flying an airplane, you will want to follow certain procedures with your Pilot to help the relationship take off smoothly. To do this, feel free to use your own personal way of relating to children your Pilot's age.

If your mentoring relationship doesn't take off immediately with your Pilot, don't take it personally. Several reasons could account for a slow take off. Some children, for example, may not easily build trust toward someone like you. You might, for example, remind your Pilot of someone in his or her past who belittled, ignored, or abandoned him/her. Another possible reason may be the Pilot's shyness. Withdrawn children, for example, may require extra Co-Pilot patience until they become more comfortable with the relationship. Other reasons a Pilot might be reluctant to bond with you are covered in Chapter 5.

Taking off in your relationship with a young person may require you to be very patient and determined. Hang in there! There are countless examples of children who eventually came around in the relationship, due to their Co-Pilots' caring and persistence. On the next pages you will find several ideas that can help you achieve a smooth take off with your Pilot.

In the Beginning

1. Clarify Expectations:

Briefly introduce yourself and give a description of a Pilot and Co-Pilot. Check out your child's understanding of and feelings toward the program. Also clarify where, when, and for how long you will be meeting together as Pilot and Co-Pilot.

2. Discuss Confidentiality:

Explain to your Pilot that you will keep private what he/she says, unless you are told about something that involves danger. Then you must tell your Program Coordinator about the situation so that you can be sure everyone will be safe.

Note that even if your Pilot shares with you information about past abuse or potential harm, you must tell your Program Coordinator. See page 37 for a sample statement you could use to explain this to your Pilot.

3. Encourage Your Pilot to Respond:

Be sure to ask your Pilot if he/she has any questions or feelings about the program. Give him/her another chance to share any curiosities or uncertainties he/she might have. Remember, if your Pilot is somewhat unresponsive, don't take it personally. Allow your relationship to develop over time.

4. Get to Know your Pilot and Have Some Fun:

In the beginning of any mentoring relationship, it is important to take things slow and easy. Be playful and have some fun times together. On the next pages, you will find lists of ice-breaking questions and activities to help your relationship take off. You may want to look through these lists again prior to your first meeting with your Pilot.

Dan

Activity 3.1: Ice-Breaking Questions

Directions: The following are sample questions you can ask your Pilot to help "break the ice" during your first few meetings. Practice asking some of these questions with other Co-Pilots in your training group.

1. What is your favorite (least favorite) kind of music? *rak* TV show? Sport? School subject? Story? Animal? Place to go? Time of year?
    science *Wolf* *Alska* *Winter*

2. What do you like to do when you are not in school? *Play Gatar*

3. If you had all the money you would need to go anywhere you wanted, where would you go? *Alska*

4. What is a special interest (or hobby) that you have?
    Play Gatar

5. What are some things that you can do very well? *play Gatar*

6. What is one thing that you wish you could learn to do better? *play Gatar*

7. What do you hope to be doing five years from now? Ten years from now?
    do construction

8. What do you look for in a friend?

9. When have you felt proud? Embarrassed? Afraid? Angry? Sad?

10. If you had a magic wand, that could change things, what would you change about the world? School? Your friends? Yourself? Your situation?

11. When have you helped someone?

12. Who is your hero/heroine? What do you like so much about this person?

13. What is one of your favorite dreams?

14. You have been selected to go on a two month expedition to search for life on Mars. You will already be taking everything you need to survive. You are allowed to choose three additional things to take with you.
    What would they be?

Other Ice Breakers

Here are some other activities that may help you and your Pilot take off in your mentoring relationship.

1. Play a sport such as basketball. Play catch with a baseball or football. If you are not skilled at these activities, but your Pilot likes them, let him/her teach you.

2. Bring some play items and let your Pilot choose which one(s) to play with. For example, bring puppets, dolls, crayons/paper, and/or clay or Play Doh®. You could also bring a bag of small plastic figures such as animals, dinosaurs, people, fences, cars, etc. To provide a special place in which your Pilot can play with these items, make a "sand tray" using a rectangular plastic container (about 18" long) and fill it half way with play sand. Children often become very expressive when encouraged to make up a story in the sand using the figures. You may want to check with your school counselor to determine if he/she has a sand tray and/or any items you can use.

3. Have breakfast or lunch with your Pilot at school.

4. Ask your Pilot if he/she would like to meet during a recess period.

5. Meet with the other Pilots and Co-Pilots in your program for group ice-breaking activities. This could take place in the school gym, cafeteria, field, or at a local recreational facility.

6. Ask your Pilot to show you a talent or interest that he/she has such as drawing, painting, playing a musical instrument, rapping, poetry, athletic skill, or making up a story.

7. Learn a magic trick and show it to your Pilot. Ask him/her to show you one. Learn a magic trick together and perform it for others.

8. Develop a "special hand-shake" with your Pilot which you will use whenever you meet. Be sure to let your Pilot help you invent it.

Landing

Sadly, every journey must come to an end. However, the ending of your Co-Piloting relationship should not be thought of as a "relationship termination." Rather, it is a "transition period." Both you and your Pilot may be sad and need to grieve in some way as your relationship nears this time. It is best if this grieving process begins well before the final meeting.

Landing can actually become a very "uplifting" experience, if approached carefully and systematically. Here is a list of suggestions that will help you and your Pilot derive the most benefit from this process.

1. **Prepare Early:** If possible, begin preparing your Pilot at least three weeks before your final meeting. Remind your Pilot periodically when your last meeting will take place.

2. **Review Highlights:** Recall some of the smooth and turbulent times during your relationship.

3. **Share Feelings Openly:** Encourage discussions about concluding your time together.

4. **Reaffirm Strengths in Each Other:** Talk about the positive qualities you found in each other during your relationship.

5. **Avoid New Issues:** Ensure that your final meeting time does not include the discussion of new issues that will need to be resolved. If your Pilot brings up a new concern, either refer him/her to your Program Coordinator, or deal with the situation and postpone your final meeting to another time. Then, try once again to "avoid new issues."

6. **Exchange Written Words:** Share with one another good-bye letters or cards. Even if your Pilot is too young to read, you may want to write or type a letter for your pilot to include in his or her "Pilot Portfolio" which is described on page 50 of this book. Read the letter to your Pilot and then help him/her to attach it in the portfolio.

7. **End on a "High:"** Be sure to laugh and have some fun during your last formal meeting together. Remember, "When saying good-bye. . . end on a high!"

Activity 3.2: Safe Landing (A Simulation)

Directions: This activity is a simulation of what it can be like to help your Pilot have a safe landing in your relationship. It works best if you have at least eight participants. If you don't have eight Co-Pilots to participate, merely read through this activity. Then discuss with your group answers to the questions in the "Follow-Up" section.

You will need some room to move around. One volunteer will become a "pilot" who will pretend to make a difficult landing on a runway. Another volunteer will become the "air-traffic controller" who is in the airport control tower attempting to help the "pilot" land safely.

All the other participants should stand in two equally long parallel lines, with each person in one line facing across towards people in the other line. This is the "airport landing strip." The "pilot" should stand between the lines at one end, and the "air-traffic controller" should stand at the opposite end in the "control tower."

Here is the story: The "pilot" is flying solo and coming in for a difficult landing. (Place a blindfold, or equivalent, over the eyes of the "pilot" to represent poor visibility). The "air-traffic controller" must talk the "pilot" down for a safe landing. The "air-traffic controller" and "pilot" can talk back-and-forth with one another (by radio). Using dialog only, the "pilot" must be guided from one side of the runway to the other, where the "co-pilot" is standing. When the "pilot" finally reaches the "air-traffic controller" a safe landing has occurred and the activity is finished.

Hints: After blindfolding the "pilot" turn him/her around about three times. Then, several people should place objects or themselves on the runway to represent debris from a storm. People nearby should ensure the "pilot" doesn't fall as he/she approaches the more difficult obstacles.

Follow-Up:
1. What was it like for the "pilot" when he/she discovered that a blindfold would be worn and that later, obstacles would be placed on the runway? How might this experience be similar to the time when your Pilot approaches the final landing of your relationship?

2. In this simulation, what were the "air traffic controller's" responsibilities? How are these similar to your responsibilities in landing your relationship with your Pilot?

3. How well did the "air-traffic controller" in this simulation reassure the "pilot?" How can you reassure your Pilot during your landing?

4. How well did the "air-traffic controller" in this simulation invite the "pilot" to communicate his or her thoughts and feelings? How can you invite your Pilot to share as you approach the landing of your relationship?

Chapter 4

Handling Turbulence

"When the going gets tough, just about all you can do is keep going forward, and press on."

Chuck Yeager*

* Chuck Yeager was a professional test pilot. Among his many accomplishments was a record breaking flight in which he was the first human being to travel faster than the speed of sound.

Handling Turbulence

Though Co-Piloting can be a very enjoyable and fulfilling experience for you and your Pilot, there may be some "turbulence" ahead. However, these challenging times can be turned into powerful opportunities to break new ground with your Pilot. Many Co-Pilots and Pilots have said that getting through a difficult time together was one of the most helpful experiences they had in the program.

When real pilots are faced with a stormy weather situation, they (along with their crew and control tower personnel) must consider the severity of the situation and their own limitations before deciding how they will proceed. In some cases, the best method to handle turbulence is to fly over or around the storm. Other times, a decision is made to patiently wait for a better time to take off. Sometimes, the pilot may fly directly into the storm knowing that he/she has the skills and support to handle the situation.

Similarly, you and your Pilot may encounter some turbulent times during your work together. When you do, you will need to consider your own limitations and have several courses of action from which to choose.

Knowing Your Limitations

You should become clearly aware of your limitations as a Co-Pilot so that you can set boundaries in your relationship with your Pilot. Unfortunately, some difficult situations may arise in which it is not clear how you should proceed. The following descriptions of Co-Pilot limitations can help you know what to do in most situations. If, after considering these limitations, you continue to feel unsure about how to proceed, you should seek guidance from your Program Coordinator, fellow Co-Pilots, or other resource people who are available to you.

1. Training: If your Pilot ever requires assistance that is beyond your skill level, you will need to know how to make appropriate referrals (see "Making Referrals" on page 46). If you encounter such a situation ask your Program Coordinator for guidance. For example, if you have not had specific training in addictions and family systems, you should not give advice on how to handle an alcoholic parent. By giving untrained advice in such cases, caring people have sometimes unknowingly contributed to the family's problems. Instead, you may want to accompany your Pilot to a first session with a counselor, social worker, or other professional who is trained in this area.

2. Confidentiality: Another critical limitation is that you may not always be able to keep everything your Pilot tells you secret. When your Pilot informs you about past, present, or potential harm to him/herself or others, it must be reported. If your Pilot tells you, for example, about being abused, you cannot keep this a secret. You must inform your Program Coordinator or other person to whom you've been directed to give this information.

One way to tell a child about your limits to confidentiality is to make a statement like the following:

> *"Anything you say in here is just between you and me. But, if you ever tell me about something dangerous to you or someone else, then I will have to tell (give the name of the Program Coordinator) about it. This is because I care about you and have to make sure you and others are safe."*

3. Time: You may find that your Pilot occasionally may not want to stop your meeting when you need to leave. In this situation, it is important to take care of your needs by setting clear boundaries for your time together. Do not let your Pilot extend your meeting time through manipulation. It may help to let your Pilot know when only five minutes remain in the session. This will provide your child with a final opportunity to cover anything else he/she would like to talk about.

4. Energy: Sometimes, your personal energy may be at a lower level than usual. When this occurs, don't force yourself to "hang in there" while trying to hide yawns. Be honest with your Pilot. Perhaps taking a walk together or moving to another location will help. If this doesn't work, end the meeting with an invitation to make up the time on another day. Ending the session like this may be disappointing to your Pilot, but your honesty can provide a valuable lesson.

5. Issue Sensitivity: Most of us have certain issues that seem to really bother us. We each have our own set of pet peeves. Be sure that your sensitivities don't interfere in your relationship with your Pilot. If you ever believe you are becoming oversensitive about some things your Pilot says or does, share this with your Co-Pilot Support Group or Program Coordinator. They can help you brainstorm some other approaches to the situation.

If your Pilot says or does something that alarms you, be careful not to overreact. Be a good listener and share your concerns about the issue with your Co-Pilot Support Group or Program Supervisor.

6. Closeness: You and your Pilot may develop close feelings toward one another. This is expected and encouraged up to a point. Discuss with your group of Co-Pilots the "do's and don'ts" of physically touching your Pilot.

In addition, we do not recommend that you take your Pilot alone to your home. Although many Co-Pilots have taken their Pilots to sporting events, shows, and shopping malls, it is safer to do this with a group. If you and your Pilot plan to meet outside of the regularly planned Co-Pilot program, check with your Program Coordinator and be sure to acquire parental/guardian permission.

Activity 4.1: Co-Pilot Limitations

Directions: Gather in a small group with other Co-Pilots. Together, develop a humorous skit in which one of you (Co-Pilot) is faced with a situation which raises one of the six Co-Pilot limitation issues just described. Be sure to involve each of your group members in the skit. Develop a clear beginning to your skit but leave the ending open, with the Co-Pilot unsure how to proceed.

Act out your skit in front of the other Co-Pilots. When finished, invite the audience to brainstorm and evaluate different approaches the Co-Pilot might have used in the situation.

Pilot Resistance

As mentioned earlier, your Pilot at some time may become resistant in your relationship. This resistance may only occur during a few meetings, or it may last a few months. If you observe this in your Pilot, be sure not to take it personally. Remember, you will be working with a child who has probably never met anyone quite like you. It may take some time for you to become comfortable with each other.

Behavioral Indicators of Resistance

The following behaviors, if they are frequently and continually observed, may indicate that your Pilot is resisting the relationship.
If these behaviors continue for more than two meetings, seek guidance from your Program Coordinator and/or Co-Pilot Support Group.

- ☐ Absent from your meetings
- ☐ Quiet and not talkative
- ☐ Uncooperative
- ☐ Oppositional body language (such as rolling his or her eyes)

Reasons Behind Pilot Resistance

If you believe your Pilot is being resistant, consider the following possible reasons:

⇨ **Mandatory or "Pushed" Involvement:** The child may resent the fact that he/she did not have much choice in the matter. This is usually more of a factor when mentoring adolescents.

⇨ **Unfamiliar Territory:** The child sees the Co-Pilot as someone who is quite different from him/her and is unsure how to relate.

⇨ **Fear of Loss:** The child is afraid to allow any relationship to develop that might result in emotional pain.

⇨ **Peer Influence:** The child is afraid that his or her peers will ridicule him/her for having a mentor.

Activity 4.2: Handling Resistance

Directions: Look through the five ways to handle Pilot resistance described on the next page. Break up into triads (groups of three) and give each group a few minutes to develop a humorous skit showing resistance. Within each triad, label one person as the "Pilot," another as the "Co-Pilot," and the third as the "Observer." Have the Pilot play the role of a mildly resistant child. He/she might begin by acting bored and frustrated with the Co-Pilot's efforts to hold a conversation about schoolwork.

Before the skit reaches its conclusion, the participants should stop and brainstorm some possible ways to approach the Pilot. The five "Tips" listed on the next page may be helpful to consider. Then, resume the skit, trying out one or more of the ideas that were discussed. Note that the person acting as the Pilot should allow the strategies to be successful.

Finally, hold a group discussion about the skit and about each of the "Tips for Handling Resistance." Brainstorm examples of when these tips might be useful with Pilots in different situations.

Tips for Handling Resistance

1. **Do More and Talk Less.** Back off from asking too many questions and invite your Pilot to do some activities with you. For example, take a walk, play catch, or play a game. Chapter 4 will provide you with several other involving activities which you can do with your Pilot.

2. **Follow the Pilot's Lead.** As much as possible, let your Pilot determine what you will be doing or talking about during your time together. Use more of a learner/follower approach rather than a leader/teacher approach, especially in the beginning of the relationship. Later, after the relationship builds, your Pilot will be more receptive to your taking the lead sometimes.

3. **Be Persistent.** Don't give up. Some Co-Pilots who became discouraged and thought of quitting the relationship, discovered that their sheer determination finally paid off. Persistence is one way that you can show your Pilot you are more genuinely caring than other "helpers" he/she has known.

4. **Try Yielding.** If working with your Pilot feels like trying to open a locked door, try "yielding." This is a term used in some martial art styles that describes a creative backing-off approach as a way to weaken an opponent's attack. You can try this backing-off from your Pilot's resisting behaviors by acknowledging your feelings of discouragement. Invite your Pilot to reveal his or her real feelings about working with you. If your Pilot discloses any feelings to you, listen to them carefully. This strategy may provide the "break through" opportunity for which you have been hoping. It can provide a new beginning in your relationship.

5. **Seek Assistance.** If all else fails, explore the situation with your Program Coordinator and/or Co-Pilot Support Group.

Tips for Handling Other Challenges

When your Pilot:

☐ **Is easily distracted during your conversations.**
Tip: Check with the Pilot's counselor, teachers, and/or parents to find out if this is typical behavior for the child. Provide feedback to your Pilot about this behavior. Then, ask what might be the reasons behind the behavior. Explore together what each of you might do differently to help improve the situation.

☐ **Resists ending your meetings.**
Tip: Together, work out some way to cue the child that there are five minutes remaining in your meeting. This could be done by using a hand signal or by telling him/her directly that the meeting is almost over. If the resistance continues, inform your Program Coordinator and/or your Co-Pilot Support Group.

☐ **Seems unappreciative of your efforts.**
Tip: Pilots should not be expected to express much appreciation for anything you do with them. Most children eventually come to deeply value their mentors. But, some children do not feel comfortable with, or know how to express these feelings.

☐ **Expresses intense emotions.**
Tip: Some children and adults are uncomfortable when someone shows emotions. When your Pilot tells or shows you about his or her feelings, always become focused and be a good listener. It is important to show caring, accepting, and a desire to understand the child's views. Try to avoid reassuring statements like "It's going to be okay" or "Tomorrow, you'll feel better about things." These statements are often interpreted as discounting their feelings about the situation. Also, avoid giving quick advice. Most children, when they express intense emotions, don't want to be told what they should do. What they want most is someone who is a caring, patient listener.

☐ Procrastinates.

Tip: All of us put things off sometimes. However, if this is a frequent behavior for your Pilot, it is probably causing problems for him/her. Ask your Pilot to work through the Self-Improvement Lessons later in this book, in particular, Lessons 1 and 7. Then help your Pilot set some short term goals that he/she can accomplish within a set amount of time. Provide an incentive to help motivate your Pilot. For example, allow your Pilot to earn extra time to participate in a special activity with you.

☐ Has low self-esteem.

Tip: Self-esteem consists of two parts, self-confidence (how capable we believe we are) and self-worth (how valuable we believe we are). To help raise your Pilot's self-confidence, you might start by focusing on Self-Improvement Lessons 1, 2, 3, and 10 in this book. But raising your Pilots self-confidence may take more than a set of activities. It may require you and others to provide a lot of encouragement and recognition over a long period of time.

To help raise self-worth, you will need to help your Pilot view him or herself as valuable and worthwhile. By simply giving your valuable time and energy, you will show your Pilot that at least someone believes that he/she has value. In addition, you will help build up your Pilot through consistent affirmations or compliments about his/her abilities (see in particular Self-Improvement Lesson 1).

☐ Seems to be holding a lot of anger inside.

Tip: Share with your Pilot your observations that led you to this impression. Then, encourage him/her to share the underlying reasons. It may help your Pilot to go through Self-Improvement Lessons 2, 3, 4, and 6. If your Pilot continues to express angry feelings, see your Program Coordinator for some other ideas.

Gets into trouble with misbehavior at school.

Tip: Don't focus most of your time together on your Pilot's behavior difficulties. Depending on your Pilot's age and abilities, help him or her first set a goal on which to work. Then brainstorm alternative approaches your Pilot could use to reach that goal. Next, encourage your Pilot to practice these different approaches by role-playing with you. You might begin by working through Self-Improvement Lessons 2, 4, 6, and 7.

Has parents or guardians who are not cooperative with your efforts.

Tip: It is important to build a positive relationship with your Pilot's parents or guardians. Some Co-Pilots visit their Pilot's homes at the beginning of the relationship while other Co-Pilots make regular home visits. Allow the parents or guardians to get to know you and encourage them to share their perspectives. Help them feel involved in your work by asking for suggestions for working with their child.

Making Referrals

When to Refer Your Pilot

There are several situations in which you should refer your Pilot immediately to the appropriate professional helper. For example, think about your potential referral sources if you discovered that your Pilot was:

- ☐ Acting out sexually.
- ☐ Involved in illegal activities with a group of older children.
- ☐ Considering running away from home.
- ☐ Being threatened by older children.
- ☐ Threatening to harm him/herself or someone else.
- ☐ Experiencing prolonged or intense fear, anger, or depression.
- ☐ Raising questions that you believe someone else could answer better than you.
- ☐ Bragging about finding a weapon.

How to Refer Your Pilot

When making a referral, you may find the following suggestions helpful:

1. Listen to your Pilot's feelings in a caring and open manner.

2. Express your personal support for the child and your concern about the situation.

3. Remind your Pilot of your limited training in dealing with this kind of situation.

4. Offer to go with your Pilot and tell about the situation to a professional helper.

5. Follow-up with your Pilot and/or referral person to ensure that assistance is being provided.

6. Continue meeting with your Pilot, listening and providing encouragement.

Activity 4.3: List of Referral Resources

Directions: Know the best person to whom you will refer your Pilot for different situations. Complete the following list of resources so you will have it at your fingertips if you ever need it.

Co-Pilot Coordinator:

_____

How to Contact:

_____

Pilot's Information:
Name:

_____

Address:

_____

_____

Phone: _____

Home Contact(s):

_____

How to Contact:

_____

_____

Other Family Contact(s):

_____

_____

_____

_____

School Information:
Address:

_____

_____

Phone: _____

Teachers:

_____

_____

Counselor:

_____

Phone: _____

Other School Contact:

_____

Community Resources:

_____

_____

_____

_____

_____

Other:

_____

_____

_____

_____

Chapter 5

Projects for You
and Your Pilot

"Tell me and I'll forget.
Show me, and I may not remember.
Involve me, and I'll understand."
Native American saying

Projects for You and Your Pilot

Once you begin meeting with your Pilot, you may want to spend a lot of your time talking together. However, some caution is important here. Be careful not to give your Pilot the impression that you are trying to be his/her teacher or parent. Too much talking may eventually result in your Pilot pulling away emotionally from you.

Ensure that you and your Pilot become involved together in some fun, meaningful activities or projects. This chapter will provide a collection of games and activities that will help you and your Pilot to have fun and memorable experiences together.

Pilot Portfolio

Use the following list to help your Pilot develop a portfolio about him/herself. You will need to acquire some kind of device for holding pages, such as a folder with pockets or a three-ring notebook with inserts. You might provide some construction paper and other art supplies which you and your Pilot can use to make the portfolio. Compiling this material is best accomplished as an ongoing activity with the periodic adding of materials.

Portfolio Contents

1. Introduction (A brief description with a photograph, if possible)
2. List of Personal Interests and Preferences (See Activity 3.1)
3. Favorite Activities
4. Abilities (See Chapter 6, Lesson 1)
5. Personal Goals
6. Successes and Accomplishments
7. Complimentary Letters About the Pilot
8. Sample Work
    • Schoolwork
    • Artwork
    • Poems
    • Song/Rap Lyrics
    • Stories
    • Photographs
    • Other Projects

60 Games and Activities for Pilots/Co-Pilots

Games

- [ ] Play non-competitive board games.
- [ ] Play computer games designed for two people.
- [ ] Do a scavenger hunt together.
- [ ] Make up a game together and play it.

Creative Arts

- [ ] Make a "Me Collage" (a collection of pictures/words that describe your Pilot).
- [ ] Design a personal coat-of-arms (with symbols that describe your Pilot).
- [ ] Make an "I Can" (a can covered with cut-out pictures of eyes from magazines) and fill it with statements about what your Pilot can do well.
- [ ] Write and/or sing a rap song about Co-Piloting.
- [ ] Make up a skit on a certain topic and present it to the class.
- [ ] Have your Pilot play his/her favorite music and discuss its meaning.
- [ ] Design and create a presentation for a school bulletin board.
- [ ] Create a display for a multicultural fair.

Sports/Athletics

- [ ] Shoot baskets (basketball).
- [ ] Play catch (baseball, football).
- [ ] Have the Pilot show or teach you about a sport or athletic skill.
- [ ] Exercise together (jog, walk, aerobics, etc.).
- [ ] Collect information about athletes and/or teams.
- [ ] Attend a sporting event together.
- [ ] Arrange for your Pilot to meet a high school, college, or professional athlete.

Service Learning

- ☐ Create a "care package" or other gift for a needy student or family.
- ☐ Volunteer together to be "Meeters and Greeters" at one or more Parent Teacher Organization meetings.
- ☐ Give time to a local animal welfare society.
- ☐ Volunteer together to provide "foster" care for an abandoned animal until a permanent home can be found for it.
- ☐ Adopt a place on the school grounds to keep clean.
- ☐ Manage a booth at a school fair or carnival.
- ☐ Plant a tree, bush, or flower.
- ☐ Adopt a nursing home resident and visit him/her weekly.
- ☐ Make a presentation to younger students about a topic such as tobacco or alcohol/drugs. Be sure the lesson is age-appropriate.
- ☐ Assist a kindergarten teacher in the classroom.
- ☐ Help your child read a story to you.
- ☐ Construct something that a teacher can use in the classroom.
- ☐ Volunteer together for a fundraising activity.
- ☐ Assist with the school store.
- ☐ Help decorate the school or other community building for a holiday.

Academic Encouragement

- ☐ Read stories together, or take turns reading to a younger child.
- ☐ Write a story together using mostly the Pilot's ideas. Or, for younger Pilots, have the child dictate a story which you write up for him or her.
- ☐ Study together (homework and test preparation).
- ☐ Take turns reading to each other (stories, newspaper/magazine articles, homework, reading assignments).
- ☐ Make a presentation together to a younger group of students about "How to Study Better."
- ☐ Develop a schedule chart for study times.
- ☐ Work together to clean out and organize Pilot's notebook(s), book bag, and/or locker (with your Pilot's permission).
- ☐ Visit the school media center or public library together.

Career Exploration

- [ ] Help out on "Career Day."
- [ ] Build a special project together and put it on display.
- [ ] Volunteer at school functions.
- [ ] Visit and interview people in various careers.
- [ ] Arrange for your Pilot to "shadow" you at your job site.
- [ ] Visit the vocational program at a nearby high school.
- [ ] Check out different kinds of careers in the school library or career center.

Other Activities

- [ ] Have your Pilot keep a "Success Journal" (a diary of daily accomplishments).
- [ ] Play together during recess.
- [ ] Cook a special meal together.
- [ ] Sew something together.
- [ ] Plan an outing or activity with the other Pilots and Co-Pilots.
- [ ] Take a walk around the playground or school yard just to talk.
- [ ] Participate in a ropes course with other Pilots and Co-Pilots.
- [ ] Have breakfast or lunch together at the school.
- [ ] Have a meal together at a restaurant.
- [ ] Learn to perform a magic trick together.
- [ ] Challenge each other to reach some personal goal.

Chapter 6

Self-Improvement Lessons for Pilots

"The future of [humankind] lies waiting for those who will come to understand their lives and take up their responsibilities to all living things."
Vine Victor Deloria, Jr.*

*Vine Victor Deloria, Jr. is an author and Native American rights leader.

Self-Improvement
Lessons for Pilots

On the following pages, you will find 11 lessons containing a total of 85 activities that you can complete with your Pilot. Each can help you discuss with your Pilot important issues in his/her life and explore various strategies for dealing with them.

Recommendations:

1. If your Pilot has the ability, encourage him/her to read some of these along with you. Occasionally stop to make sure that your Pilot is understanding what you are reading. Once you have read over an activity, discuss the information together.

2. Activities in each of the 11 lessons provide opportunities for you and your Pilot to share your feelings, beliefs, and ideas on a variety of important issues. Be open and honest with your views while being a good listener as your Pilot expresses his/her opinions.

3. Use these lessons occasionally, not during every meeting. Remember that these lessons should not become the primary work you do with your Pilot. They are intended to help you both focus on some important aspect of personal development. Instead, use the lessons to help start discussions on the topics. Then, encourage your Pilot to explore how the information relates to him/herself.

4. Don't worry too much about the sequence in which you cover these lessons with your Pilot. You and/or your Pilot may select lessons that seem most interesting or relevant.

5. Feel free to slow down and take extra time with some activities. You might find that something you are covering provides a timely learning opportunity for your Pilot.

6. Your Pilot may want to include some of the products of these activities in his/her Pilot Portfolio.

THE ELEVEN LESSONS
(Containing 85 activities)

1. "My Abilities" (Activities 1-9)

2. "My Attitudes" (Activities 10-18)

3. "My Feelings" (Activities 19-25)

4. "My Anger" (Activities 26-33)

5. "My Friends" (Activities 34-41)

6. "My Conflicts with Others"
(Activities 42-48)

7. "My Confidence with Schoolwork"
(Activities 49-54)

8. "My Understanding of Alchohol"
(Activities 55-59)

9. "My Understanding of Other Drugs"
(Activities 60-66)

10. "My Character" (Activities 67-75)

11. "My Future Career" (Activities 76-85)

LESSON 1: "MY ABILITIES"

Helping a child feel lovable and capable are two important goals of mentoring children. One way to approach this is to determine some of the abilities your Pilot has, then to provide continuing affirmations of these abilities to him/her.

A. Identifying Abilities

Every child has a unique combination of personal strengths or abilities. To identify these, you might interview the child's teacher, parents, counselor, peers, or others who might know him/her. Try to determine at least five special abilities your Pilot has and write them down. Ask your Pilot to tell you what he/she can do well, and add these words to your list. As you become familiar with your Pilot, you might notice other abilities that you want to add to your list.

Activity 1: Use the "Ability Words Checklist"

Grades K-5
Materials: A copy of the following "Ability Words"

The following list of "Ability Words" can help you find the best terms to describe your Pilot. As you discover new words that may apply to your Pilot, place a check next to them on the list, or write them on this page. Note that even though some of these words may be beyond the vocabulary of your child, he/she may enjoy learning them anyway. Help your Pilot learn his/her own list of ability words. Note that for Pilots in grades K-2, look over this list in advance to identify which words might be most appropriate for their vocabulary level.

Ability Words

☐ Adventurous	☐ Determined	☐ Hard Worker	☐ Resourceful
☐ Appreciative	☐ Eager	☐ Helpful	☐ Respectful
☐ Artistic	☐ Energetic	☐ Honest	☐ Sensitive
☐ Athletic	☐ Fair	☐ Leader	☐ Sharing
☐ Brave	☐ Faithful	☐ Loving	☐ Thoughtful
☐ Bright	☐ Flexible	☐ Loyal	☐ Trustworthy
☐ Calm	☐ Forgiving	☐ Motivated	☐ Unselfish
☐ Caring	☐ Friendly	☐ Neat	
☐ Careful	☐ Funny	☐ Open-Minded	_____
☐ Cooperative	☐ Generous	☐ Organized	
☐ Creative	☐ Gentle	☐ Patient	_____
☐ Curious	☐ Giving	☐ Positive	
☐ Dependable	☐ Good Sport	☐ Prepared	_____

B. Affirming Abilities

Once a few words have been identified to describe some of your Pilot's abilities, use one or more of the following strategies. These suggestions will provide you with different ways to make affirmations to your Pilot. They will also help your Pilot learn to use self-talk to affirm him/herself.

Activity 2: Make an "I Can"

Grades K-5

Materials: Empty soup can, magazines/newspapers, two pairs of scissors, glue/paste.

An "I Can" is an emptied soup-sized can with one end open. Work with your Pilot to cut out as many pictures of large eyes as you can. Don't cut just around the outline of the eyes, cut a larger circle around each. Sometimes, cut both eyes out in one piece. Note that animal and cartoon eyes can be included and will add more variety to the look of the can.

With your Pilot, paste the pictures around the can until it is covered with the eyes. Now you have a can coated with eyes— an "I Can." When finished, you and your Pilot should partially fill the can with small objects or pictures of things that represent his/her unique combination of abilities. You may also look for ability words in magazines, cut them out, and place them in the can. Later, you or your Pilot might empty out the contents of the can on a table and review the collection of his/her ability words and symbols. Other times, you and your Pilot might look in the can for one or two particular abilities that might help him/her to have more confidence in a certain situation.

Activity 3: Make an "Ability Bag"
Grades K-5
Materials: Paper bag, magazines/newspapers, two pairs of scissors,
glue/paste.

Similar to the "I Can," an ability bag will contain objects, pictures, and words that describe your Pilot's abilities. The bag has the advantage of being larger, so it can hold larger objects. Almost any size paper bag will work. The bag can also be drawn on or decorated by the Pilot. His/her name may be colored or painted on it. Look through magazines and/or newspapers with your Pilot and paste on pictures that describe him/her. You might suggest how some pictures remind you of him/her, but your Pilot should have the final decision as to what is pasted on the bag.

Activity 4: Play "Toilet Paper Brainstorm"
Grades K-5
Materials: One roll of toilet paper.

Have your Pilot unwind some toilet paper from a roll. Then, have him/her tear off individual sections of the paper he/she has taken from the roll. Each time a section is torn off, the Pilot has to tell about one of his/her abilities by completing the sentence, "I can . . . ."

Activity 5: Sing the "Ability Song"
Grades K-2
Materials: None

The Ability Song consists of made-up lyrics that describe your Pilot's particular abilities. It follows the tune of "Are You Sleeping." Use the following example to help you develop your song. Note that the song can be repeated for most, or all of your Pilot's ability words. You might want to write your Pilot's lyrics down for future reference.

"I know Jennifer."	*Pilot echoes*
"She is friendly."	*Pilot echoes*
"It's easy to like her."	*Pilot echoes*
"She has a big smile."	*Pilot echoes*

Activity 6: Play "Show Me Your Ability"
Grades K-5
Materials: None

Once you know some words that identify your Pilot's abilities, think of some ways he/she might be able to demonstrate each ability to you through play. As your Pilot shows you an ability, say something like, "Wow! You sure are showing your _____ (ability word)." The following are some examples of ways your Pilot could show you abilities through play:

Ability	Have your Pilot:
Adventurous:	Be the leader while taking you for a walk.
Brave:	Perform in a play or skit.
Caring:	Make a gift for another person.
Creative:	Draw/paint a picture, or make up a story/rap song.
Friendly:	Introduce you to one of his/her friends.
Funny:	Tell you a funny story or joke.
Helpful:	Assist someone while you watch.
Organized:	Show you his/her desk, locker, or notebook.
Sensitive:	Put on two puppets and make up a story showing how one understands the feelings of the other.
Trustworthy:	Cover your eyes with your hands and allow your Pilot to take you for a short "blind" walk.

Other Activities

Activity 7 *(Grades K-5):* Go with your Pilot to meet some of the people who know him/her. Ask them to tell you about your Pilot's abilities in front of him/her. You might want to talk with these people before bringing your Pilot to them. Let them know some of the ability words you have identified for your Pilot and ask them if they have any others to add to your list.

Activity 8 *(Grades K-5):* Find one or more stories that provide examples of abilities which your Pilot possesses. If your Pilot can't read yet, read the stories to him/her. Otherwise, read the stories together. Explore how the stories relate to your Pilot's abilities.

Activity 9 *(Grades K-5):* Identify one or more careers in which your Pilot's abilities are valued. Then, take your Pilot to see the people working in that field. Emphasize how your Pilot's abilities would be helpful in the job. If taking a trip to a job site is not possible, conduct a phone interview, read about the career in a book, or use the internet to search for relevant information.

LESSON 2: "MY ATTITUDE"

Children's attitudes reflect how they view themselves. When a child has low self-esteem, he/she will likely have a negative attitude toward others. For example, children with low self-esteem may make very negative comments about their teachers, family members, and peers.

Helping a child change his/her attitude is not easy. One might begin by teaching children what the term "attitude" means and how positive and negative attitudes differ from each other. Then, they might benefit from exploring and practicing different situations in which they can change their attitudes from negative to positive.

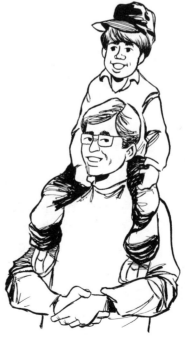

Activity 10: Understanding Negative and Positive Attitudes

Grades K-5
Materials: None

Read the following four situations, one at a time, to your Pilot. Have him/her make a frown each time he/she hears a "negative attitude" and a smile each time he/she hears a "positive attitude." When you have completed the list, make up other situations and have your Pilot respond to each with a smile or frown, or with the words "positive attitude" or "negative attitude." Afterwards, have your Pilot describe some situations to you while you frown, smile, or guess which kind of attitude he/she is describing.

- ➪ A boy gets into trouble with the teacher and throws his books on the floor.
- ➪ A girl walks up to a new student in school and asks if she wants to play with her.
- ➪ A girl tells her friends that she is not going to play with them anymore.
- ➪ A boy gets a low grade on a test, but says he's going to work hard to do better on the next test.

Activity 11: Wear "Attitude Glasses"*

Grades K-5
Materials: One pair of Sunglasses

Tell your Pilot that a positive attitude is like putting on "rose-colored glasses." Pull out a pair of sunglasses. Explain that when things are upsetting to you, you can look at these things differently and find something positive about them. Show your Pilot how someone can change a negative attitude into a positive one by telling the following situations while you either wear or don't wear the glasses.

Glasses off: "I really hate this school and everyone in it!"
Glasses on: "I get upset sometimes at school, but I like it when my teacher says something nice to me."

Glasses off: "No one in this school wants to be my friend."
Glasses on: "I need to do more things that will help others see me as a friendly person."

Glasses off: "I'll never do well in my schoolwork. I'm just a loser!"
Glasses on: "No matter what has happened in the past, I know that I can be a winner in school!"

---

* Adapted from an activity developed by Dr. Linda Myrick, Adjunct Professor, University of Florida.

Activity 12: Make an "Attitude Collage"
Grades K-5
Materials: Construction paper, magazines/newspapers, two pairs of scissors, glue/paste.

Place two pieces of construction paper on the table. Title one, "Positive Attitudes" and the other "Negative Attitudes." Work together with your Pilot to cut out pictures from magazines and/or newspapers of people who look like they have positive or negative attitudes. Positive attitude pictures are pasted on one collage, while negative attitude pictures are pasted on the other. Then talk about the difference between the two collages.

Activity 13: Change a Puppet's Attitude
Grades K-3
Materials: At least two hand puppets.

Have your Pilot choose two puppets, one for him/herself and the other for you to put on your hand. Make up a story in which your puppet has a negative attitude toward someone or something. Perhaps use one or more of the "Glasses Off" situations from Activity 11. Ask your Pilot's puppet to say or do something that will help your puppet have a more positive attitude about the situation.

Activity 14: Draw the Attitudes
Grades K-5
Materials: Crayons, drawing paper.

Have your Pilot use crayons to make two drawings about situations he/she has seen in school. The first drawing should show someone with a positive attitude and the second, someone with a negative attitude. Ask your Pilot to tell you about what happened in each situation.

Another drawing could be of a cartoon character with a positive attitude and another with a negative attitude. Then, have your Pilot tell you his/her story about the characters' attitudes. Ask him/her how the negative character could be helped to have a more positive attitude.

Activity 15: Show Thumbs-Up or Thumbs-Down

Grades K-5
Materials: None

Read each of the following items to your Pilot and add more of your own if you wish. Ask your Pilot to give a thumbs-up or thumbs-down to each. Thumbs-up means that he/she has a positive attitude toward it, whereas thumbs-down means that he/she has a negative attitude toward it. Record your Pilot's answers by placing an up or down arrow in the space before each item.

⬆ = Positive Attitude   ⬇ = Negative Attitude

☐ Your school

☐ How you look

☐ Your voice

☐ Your dreams (hopes)

☐ Your teacher

☐ School lunch

☐ Getting up in the morning

☐ Going home after school

☐ Playing with your friends

☐ Taking a test in school

☐ How you are dressed

☐ Thinking about what will happen to you next year

Other Activities

Activity 16 *(Grades K-5):* Have your Pilot identify stories about characters with negative or positive attitudes. You might also identify other stories that show attitudes and read them to him/her.

Activity 17 *(Grades K-5):* Have your Pilot tell, write, draw, or act out something he/she did that day that showed a negative or positive attitude.

Activity 18 *(Grades K-5):* When you notice your Pilot having a negative attitude, help him/her see the situation from a positive perspective.

LESSON 3: "MY FEELINGS"

"Feelings aren't good or bad, they just are." This statement holds a lot of wisdom people of all ages. Unfortunately, many children are taught that some feelings are "good" or "positive" while other feelings are "bad" or "negative." As a result, some children develop the belief that some feelings are bad or wrong to have. They become discouraged from feeling angry, sad, or scared. Some little boys, for example, are discouraged by their families and/or classmates from crying or showing that they are afraid. They are told, "Men don't cry" or "Don't be a cry baby." Little girls, on the other hand, are sometimes discouraged from admitting or showing angry feelings. They are told, "That's not nice. You shouldn't feel that way about (him, her, or me)."

Boys and girls should learn that it is alright to feel sad, scared, or angry. It's how someone **shows** these feelings that may be okay or not okay. For example, it is alright for someone to feel angry, but there are right and wrong ways to express this feeling. The following activities will help your Pilot learn about feelings. They will also encourage your Pilot to tell you more about his or her feelings with you.

Activity 19: Name the Animal's Feeling

Grades K-3
Materials: One or more stuffed animals or hand puppets.

Hold the stuffed animal or puppet and have it tell the Pilot about an emotional situation, then ask the child to guess the feelings. The following are some examples of situations:

- A pig doesn't think that other animals understand that it is actually very smart and clean, too. (sad, lonely, not liked)

- A turtle just won a race. (happy, proud, excited)

- A lion is shaking because it knows that hunters are nearby. (scared,worried, afraid)

- A dog is lying on the floor, wagging its tail when it sees you. (friendly, happy, excited)

- A mother alligator is upset because someone is getting too close to the eggs in her nest. (angry, mad, worried)

- A cat is purring and rubbing against your legs. (happy, loving, content)

Activity 20: Drawing Me With Happy and Upset Feelings

Grades K-5
Materials: Crayons and drawing paper.

Have the Pilot draw him/herself being "happy" on one piece of paper, and "upset" on another piece of paper. Then, ask him/her questions such as:

- How would someone know by looking at your picture, if you were having happy (or upset) feelings?

- What is something that makes you feel as happy (upset) as you appear to be in your picture?

Activity 21: Sing (or Rap) a Song about Feelings

Grades K-5
Materials: One copy of the song.

I Have Lots of Feelings and They're Okay *

I have lots of feelings and they're okay.
They jump up inside me every day.
If I was the President, I would say,
I have lots of feelings and they're okay.

I feel happy when I'm with my friends,
And I feel happy when the school day ends.
And I feel happy when I get to play,
'Cause happy is a feeling and it's okay.

I feel sad when I say good-bye,
And I feel sad when a bird can't fly.
And I feel sad when it rains all day,
But sad is a feeling and it's okay.

I feel proud when I bake a cake,
And I feel proud of my new pet snake.
And I feel proud when I stand and say,
"Proud is a feeling and it's okay."

I feel scared when my snake gets out,
Mom doesn't know it yet, but she'll find out.
And when she does, maybe then I'll say,
(shout) "Mom, scared is a feeling and it's okay!"

I have lots of feelings and they're okay,
They jump up inside me every day.
If I was the President, I would say,
I have lots of feelings and they're okay.

* Lyrics and music by Robert P. Bowman, Copyright, 1997 (Copied with permission)

Activity 22: Point to the Feeling Faces

Grades K-5
Materials: One copy of the "Feeling Faces."

Show the feeling faces on this page to your Pilot and ask him/her to point to the face that best shows how he/she would feel in each of the following situations. Brainstorm words that describe each feeling.

1. Someone is telling lies about you.

2. Your teacher tells you that you did a good job on your school work.

3. A dog that you don't know begins growling at you.

4. You are leaving your home in the morning to go to school.

5. You are leaving school to go back home.

6. Someone steals your dessert.

7. It's time for lunch.

8. Someone tells you that they want to beat you up.

9. Someone asks you to play with them.

10. You see an animal that is hurt.

Feeling Faces

Other Activities

Activity 23 *(Grades K-5):* Ask your Pilot to find books or magazines in the school media center that show different feelings. Read the stories to your Pilot or have him/her read them to you. Identify the different feelings as you read along.

Activity 24 *(Grades K-5):* Ask your Pilot to look in a mirror. As you name different feelings, have him/her practice showing each with his/her face.

Activity 25 *(Grades K-5):* Provide some crayons and drawing paper for your Pilot. Then ask him/her to draw designs to show the following feelings, with one feeling shown on each page.

- Happy
- Angry
- Peaceful

- Sad
- Excited
- Scared

LESSON 4: "MY ANGER"

Anger is one feeling that some children, adolescents, and adults don't handle very well. It is a secondary emotion that usually follows feelings of hurt or frustration. Children can benefit by learning about anger and nonviolent strategies that they can use when they become angry. Ask your Pilot to tell about what each of the following children are doing to "let their anger out."

Activity 26: How "Hot" do I Get?

Grades K-5
*Materials: One copy of the "Anger Thermometers" and a red crayon,
magic marker, pencil, or pen.*

Show your Pilot the empty "Anger Thermometers" below. Then present one
of the following situations to your Pilot and ask him/her to color in the
thermometer to show how angry he/she would become. Explain that more
anger is "hotter" and should be shown with higher temperatures. For younger
children you may have to show how to color the thermometers to show
different temperatures. Repeat this activity for the five situations below.

How "hot" do you get when:
1. You get <u>blamed</u> for something you didn't do?
2. Someone doesn't keep their <u>promise</u> to you?
3. You can't find your <u>pencil</u>?
4. Someone laughs at you and calls you <u>names</u>?
5. Someone accidentally knocks you <u>down</u>?

Anger Thermometer

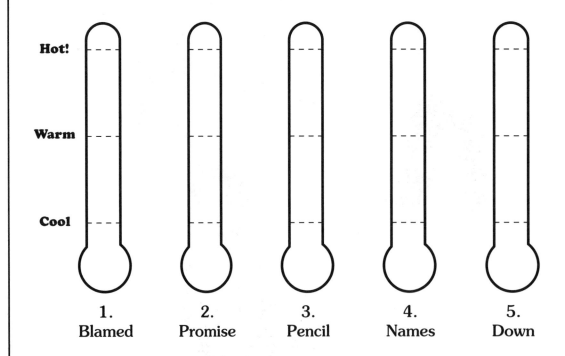

Activity 27: Things That "Bug" Me

Grades K-3
Materials: Clay or Play Doh®, glue or paste.

Have the Pilot make three or four little bugs out of some form of modeling clay (or Play Doh®). When finished, place each bug at the top of a page of drawing paper. Then ask your Pilot to draw on each page something that really bothers or "bugs" him/her. When finished, use glue to attach the bugs permanently to the pages.

An alternative way to do this activity is to have your Pilot hold one of his/her clay bugs in one hand. While looking at this bug, the Pilot should tell one thing that "bugs" him/her. When finished, the Pilot should smash the clay figure in his/her hand. Note that this alternative can be fun and cathartic for children.

Activity 28: Try to Get Out of This One

Grades K-5
Materials: One "Fingercuffs."

Purchase "Fingercuffs" which are sold in some amusement stores, though they are sometimes referred to by other names. Most people have seen Fingercuffs—they are like handcuffs for two of your fingers. A Fingercuff is a woven tube that, when a finger is placed in each end, will resist letting you pull your fingers back out. The solution is to push the fingers closer together to make the tube expand slightly in diameter. Then, the fingers can be removed easily.

Help your Pilot see that this is like anger. When you become very upset, it is best to try to relax before trying to work out the situation.

Activity 29: Practice Letting My Anger Out

Grades K-5

Materials: One wadded up piece of paper, clay or Play Doh®, and/or small soft ball.

Tell your Pilot some of the positive ways you let your anger out. Then, have your Pilot practice some of the following strategies:

- ☛ Squeeze something like a ball of wadded up paper, clay like material, or a very soft ball.
- ☛ Press your hands tightly together.
- ☛ Say to yourself over and over again, "I can be calm."
- ☛ Take two slow deep breaths.
- ☛ Count to ten before doing anything.
- ☛ Walk away and then think about something good you can do.
- ☛ Talk with someone about what made you so mad.
- ☛ Exercise, if possible.

Activity 30: Don't Let Your Anger Blow Up

Grades K-5
Materials: One deflated balloon.

Explain to your Pilot that when a student is sleeping in the morning, he/she is relaxed and not experiencing anger. Suddenly, the alarm goes off and the student's anger may start (blow a little into the balloon). Then, someone in the family yells at the student for not getting out of bed right away (inflate the balloon a little more). Next, the student misses the school bus and gets wet because it starts to rain (inflate more). Then, when the student gets to school, the teacher becomes upset because the student is tardy again (inflate more). During lunch, they serve the student's least favorite meal, boiled turkey gizzards (inflate more). Then hold the balloon so no air escapes and stop the activity.

Ask the Pilot to tell you what is eventually going to happen with the balloon if you keep adding more air. Then ask how this is like someone who becomes more and more angry.

Ask the Pilot what the student in the story could have done to let some of the anger out, without hurting anyone. Read the following list of possibilities to your Pilot and ask whether it is a good or bad idea for the student to help let out his/her anger. After each good idea, release a little air out of the balloon to show that the idea helped to release pressure. After each bad idea blow air into the balloon.

What if the student:
→ Started a fight?
→ Breathed deeply and counted to ten?
→ Kicked the wastepaper basket in the classroom?
→ Talked with the teacher or school counselor about it?
→ Talked with a friend about it?
→ Yelled at the teacher?
→ Remembered that he/she was really a good person?

Other Activities

Activity 31 *(Grades K-5):* Ask your Pilot to make up a rap song with you about anger and its consequences. Then, record it and/or perform it for younger students.

Activity 32 *(Grades K-5):* Monitor your Pilot's angry behavior by staying in close communication with his/her teacher, parent, and/or guardian. Set a goal with your Pilot for improving his/her methods of coping with anger. Offer incentives to your Pilot for improvements.

Activity 33 *(Grades K-5):* Take a trip to a local martial arts program. In particular, seek a program that features violence prevention and does not overemphasize competition.

LESSON 5: "MY FRIENDS"

Learning about how to start, sustain, and end friendships are important tasks for children to learn. Corporate personnel directors consistently agree that the most important ability new employees should possess is the capacity to relate positively with others. As young as possible, children should begin working on their social competencies. In mastering these competencies, they learn important life skills such as how to make new friends, work and play cooperatively with their peers, express their feelings and beliefs appropriately, listen accurately and sensitively to others, and cope with the loss of a friend.

Activity 34: What is a Friend?
Grades K-5
Materials: None

Ask your Pilot some or all the following questions about friendship. As your Pilot answers each question, repeat back what he/she says to allow your Pilot to reflect on what was said. When you have finished, share your own answers to some of the questions. Perhaps you can allow the Pilot to interview you.

- Who is one of your friends? What do you like to do together?
- What do you look for in a friend?
- How do you make a new friend?
- If a new student came to your class and you wanted to be friends, what could you do?
- When did a friend make you mad? Scared?
- When have you had something funny happen with a friend?
- How can you show a pet that you are its friend?
- If you could have all the friends you wanted, how many would you have?
- When have you lost a friend? What happened? How did you finally get over it?

Activity 35: Who is Your Friend?
Grades K-5
Materials: None

If you can, have your Pilot introduce you to one of his/her friends. Talk or play with both children for awhile. Then, ask them each to answer some of the questions in the previous activity. You might ask them to answer some of the questions about each other.

When finished, have the two children show you or tell you about something they like to do together. Listen attentively and summarize for them some of the qualities of friendship that you are hearing or seeing between them.

Activity 36: Develop a "Special Handshake"
Grades K-5
Materials: None

Let your Pilot help you invent a handshake that is special between you. Keep it simple and have fun. This handshake can become your own special way to greet, congratulate, and say good-bye to one another. The following are some examples of secret handshakes children have shared with their mentors.

- **Handshake from the Heart**
  Grasp each other's hand and begin little pulse-like squeezes to simulate a heartbeat.

- **Handshake Earthquake**
  Grasp hands and shake with a slight rumble between your hands.

- **Street Shake**
  Develop a series of three or four different moves that involve different ways of touching each others hands. For example, touch index fingers, then the backs of each other's thumbs, then grab each other's thumb with a single shake. Perhaps end with a "high five." Your Pilot will enjoy helping you invent this.

- **Handshake With Sound Effects**
  Invent some kind of sound that you each make while touching each others hands.

- **Finger Shake**
  Like with the "Street Shake," this one involves a series of different steps. But, the "Finger Shake" is done completely with different combinations of contacts between fingers.

Activity 37: Feel the Warmth of Friendship
Grades K-5
Materials: None

Place one of your hands in front of you at about shoulder level. Place your palm forward, and ask your Pilot to place his/her palm facing yours, about 12 inches away. Tell the child that this game is called "Feeling the Warmth of Friendship." Each of you should stare at each other's face while moving your hand forward toward your partner's hand. Stop just before your hands touch. When your hand is about a half-inch away from your Pilot's hand, you both should feel a sudden surge of warmth from each other.

Put your hands down and talk with your Pilot about how a friendship can be like this. Also, you can relate the phrase "reach out to someone in friendship." Discuss how both people must reach towards each other if a friendship is to develop warm feelings in both people.

Activity 38: Hand Mirroring

Grades K-5
Materials: None

This activity teaches children about the nature of listening and talking with others in a friendly way. It is a good follow-up to the previous activity because it is also based on an interaction between you and your Pilot using your hands.

Sit facing one another and place your hands in positions similar to the beginning of the activity "Feel the Warmth of Friendship." This time, place your hands about three inches from the child's hands. Then tell your Pilot that you are going to move your hands around and you want him/her to try to mirror or copy your hand movements with his/her hands. However, he/she should keep looking at your face during the activity, not at your hands.

Begin with slow, smooth hand movements, then increase the challenge with more animated, creative movements. Once finished, reverse roles and try to follow your Pilot's hand movements.

Discuss with your Pilot the importance of learning to lead and follow in a friendship. For example, there are times when you will want your friend to listen to you. So, you will take the lead and you will want your friend to follow what you say. On the other hand, when your friend has something to tell you, you should be a good listener and try to follow his/her lead.

In addition, ask your Pilot where each of you were looking during the activity. The answer is, at the face of the other person. Explain that this is what you should be doing when your friend is telling you something. You should be a good listener and look into his/her face to show that you are paying attention and that you are interested in what your friend is saying.

Other Activities

Activity 39 *(Grades K-5):* Ask your Pilot to draw a picture of the two of you working and/or playing together. Perhaps your Pilot can paste or tape this picture in his/her Pilot Portfolio.

Activity 40 *(Grades K-5):* Have someone take photos of you and your Pilot doing things together. Once developed, have your Pilot paste or tape the photos in his/her Pilot Portfolio.

Activity 41 *(Grades K-5):* Talk about a time when your Pilot felt like he/she lost a friend. Explore with him/her different ways people grieve and that during these times it is okay to feel sad and hurt feelings for awhile. Explain that you have never really lost a friend because you can always bring them back in your thoughts.

LESSON 6: "MY CONFLICTS WITH OTHERS"

Having conflicts with others is an inevitable part of life. Unless you choose to live the remainder of your life as a hermit, you will have to face occasional disputes with other people. Our successes or failures in handling these disputes depend in part on our mastery of skills and techniques of conflict resolution.

Children begin learning how to deal with conflicts as soon as they begin interacting with other people. By the time they enter kindergarten, some children have much better abilities to handle conflicts than others. Elementary schools are offering increasing opportunities for children to learn and practice conflict resolution strategies.

Activity 42: Open My Fist!
Grades 2-5
Materials: None

Make a fist with one of your hands and hold it out in front of your Pilot. Then invite him/her to try to get your hand open in 30 seconds. Most children will try, at first, to use force and try to pry your fingers open. However, this can be very difficult to do and usually doesn't succeed. The more force they apply to your hand, the tighter you will probably grip your fingers together.

Afterwards, talk with your Pilot about what happened. Help him/her understand that when you are trying to get someone to do something, force doesn't usually work very well. For older students, you might draw a parallel between trying to force someone's hand open and trying to pressure someone to open up to your point of view.

Next, brainstorm with your Pilot other methods that might have a better chance of opening your hand. The following are some examples:

- Asking politely (inviting)
- Tickling (using humor)
- Offering to shake hands (changing the topic)
- Offering an incentive (rewarding)

Allow your Pilot to choose a method other than force to open your fist. Then allow this method to succeed as your Pilot tries it on you. Talk about how different methods can be more effective than force, when you want to try to work out a conflict with someone else.

Activity 43: Magnetic Fingers
Grades 2-5
Materials: None

In this activity have your Pilot make a fist with each of his/her hands. Then, the two fists should be placed together, wrist-to-wrist with thumbs on the upper side of each hand. Ask your Pilot to extend his/her two index fingers to point away from the body. Then, he/she should begin pressing these two fingers against each other tightly. After about 30 seconds of pressing, ask the Pilot to slightly separate the two fingers by about one inch, while keeping the fists together.

Children are amazed to see that their two fingers seem to move back together slowly on their own, almost as if they had magnetic attraction. Teach your Pilot that this is like a conflict between two people. During some conflicts, people keep trying to use force against each other. But, if they would each separate for awhile, relax and take some time to listen to each other, then they would find that their ideas might come together without force.

Activity 44: Sometimes, You Can't Take It Back
Grades K-5
Materials: One tube or pump of toothpaste and a piece of paper or cardboard.

Ask your Pilot to squeeze or pump out a pile of toothpaste onto a piece of paper or cardboard. He/she will enjoy doing this, but will wonder why. Then, ask your Pilot to try to put all that toothpaste back into the tube. He/she will have fun trying to do this, but will discover that this is impossible to accomplish.

Ask your Pilot, "How is the toothpaste like words that you might say to others when you are angry, that you wish you hadn't said?" Explore how we sometimes might say things that we later wish we could take back, but can't. It is important, especially when you are upset with someone, to think about what you are going to say before you say it.

Activity 45: Work Out the Conflict

Grades K-5

Materials: None

Read the following situations one at a time to your Pilot. Then, discuss different ways, positive and negative, that the people could try to work out the conflict.

Conflict 1: On their way to lunch, two students start arguing about who should be first in line.

Conflict 2: Carla and Jamie had been best friends. One day Jamie started playing with another girl and Carla felt left out. Carla became angry and started a fight with the other girl.

Conflict 3: Anthony came back to his class and found his new pencils missing. He blamed Cedrick for stealing them because of what some other students said. That afternoon, Anthony took something out of Cedrick's desk to get even.

Conflict 4: Cassandra was shy and did not have many friends. Two girls in her class picked on her every day. Cassandra told the teacher and the two girls were punished. After school, the two girls came up to her and told her that they were going to "get her" on the bus. Cassandra was too afraid to get on the bus.

Conflict 5: Pete wanted to use the classroom computer. Another student had been using it for a long time, and wouldn't let Pete have a turn. Pete became angry and turned off the computer, erasing what the student had been working on.

Conflict 6: Allison's sister kept wearing her clothes without asking her. This time, she took one of Allison's favorite shirts and accidentally ripped it.

Conflict 7: A group of boys met after school. One boy wanted the group to play basketball. Another boy wanted the group to go to his home to see his new video game. A third boy wanted the group to go with him to the store to steal something.

Other Activities

Activity 46 *(Grades 3-5):* Meet with other Pilots and their Co-Pilots. As a group, develop a skit about conflicts and conflict resolution. Present the skit in front of one or more classrooms in the school. After the skit, each Pilot and Co-Pilot could meet with a small group of students and discuss positive ways of handling different conflicts.

Activity 47 *(Grades 3-5):* Encourage your Pilot to become a member of the school's peer mediation program. If the school does not have such a program, talk with your Program Coordinator about how you might support the development of such a program in the school.

Activity 48 *(Grades 3-5):* Interview several people about a time when each of them positively handled a conflict they had with another person. Be sure to interview a variety of people such as students, teachers, counselor, the principal, parents, custodians, food service workers, and/or a school secretary.

LESSON 7: "MY CONFIDENCE WITH SCHOOLWORK"

One factor that determines a child's ability to be successful with schoolwork is his/her self-confidence. Children who consistently do well in school have their self-confidence regularly reinforced. Children who consistently fail to succeed with their schoolwork eventually become discouraged and may come to believe that it is hopeless for them to be successful.

Children with low self-confidence need a lot of understanding and encouragement. They need someone to help them learn that, in spite of past failures, they will always retain the potential to succeed. As Co-Pilots to these children, you can encourage them to realize that they have many personal strengths they can use to help them with their schoolwork. In addition, there are several easy-to-learn study tricks that can help them apply their strengths more effectively to their schoolwork.

Activity 49: Four Steps to Being a "Winner" in School *

Grades K-5
Materials: One copy of "Four Winning Steps"

Help your Pilot learn that there are four steps to being a winner in school (see below and the next page). Then, encourage your Pilot to show you how he/she can use each step with actual schoolwork.

1. "I can **be** a winner"

2. "I can **show** I'm a winner"

3. "I can **start** like a winner"

4. "I can **finish** like a winner"

* From Peer Pals by Bowman and Chanaca (AGS, 1994).

Four Winning Steps

1. **"I can *be* a winner!"** You have to believe deep inside of yourself that you can feel good about your work in school.

2. **"I can *show* I'm a winner!"** You will need to show your teacher and other students that you are trying to do your very best with your schoolwork.

3. **"I can *start* like a winner!"** Learn how to get ready for your work.

4. **"I can *finish* like a winner!"** Learn how to "hang in there" and finish your work with your best effort.

Activity 50: Keys to Becoming a Confident Learner

Grades 3-5

Materials: One photocopy of "The Five Keys to Success" (on the next page).

Give your Pilot a copy of the next page of this book. Explain that he/she should practice these keys with schoolwork. Help your Pilot learn each key. Then have him/her bring you some current school work. Encourage your Pilot to talk about how each key could be used with this schoolwork.

The Five Keys to Success

Key #1: **Set a few new goals at a time.** Make these goals easy to accomplish in a short amount of time.

Key #2: **Picture yourself being successful.** Picture in your mind what it will be like when you reach your goals. Remember to think of this picture whenever you begin to feel frustrated or discouraged.

Key #3: **Control your inner voice.** Unfortunately, we sometimes say things to ourselves that discourage us. Change these negative messages to more positive ones like the following:

Negative Self-Messages	**Positive Self-Messages**
"I just can't do this work."	"I can do this work."
"I will never be able to do this."	"I will be able to do this."
"I will never be good at this."	"I can keep improving."
"I know I'm going to fail this."	"I'm going to do my best."

Key #4: **Reward your accomplishments.** When you know you have reached a short-term goal, or when you know you have done your best, treat yourself to something special.

Key #5: **Encourage others.** You may notice someone else who becomes discouraged about school. When this happens, listen to his/her feelings. Then, offer some positive suggestions such as how he/she might find a tutor. When you help others learn to think more positively, it can have a positive effect on you too!

Activity 51: "How Confident Am I?"

Grades 4-5

Materials: One copy of "Study Habits and Skills Checklist."

Study Habits and Skills Checklist

Here is a list for you to look through and discuss with your Pilot. Begin by reading through each item together. Then ask your Pilot to rate him/herself on each item.

| 1 = Poor | 3 = So-So | 4 = Good |
| 2 = Not So Good | | 5 = Excellent |

Classroom Effectiveness

_____ **Keep Good Attendance:** Missing too much school puts you behind in your work.

_____ **Set High Goals:** Believe in your ability to keep improving in your work.

_____ **Show a Winning Attitude:** Show your teacher and classmates that you are trying your best in your work.

_____ **Listen Carefully:** Pay close attention to everything the teacher says.

_____ **Take Good Notes:** Learn to write down what the teacher says.

Memorizing Facts

_____ **Use Acronyms:** Take the first letter of each term you want to memorize. Then make a nonsense word out of it. Or, you could create a new sentence with the same first letters for each word. For example, to memorize our planets in order from the sun, you can use the following statement (the first letter of each word corresponds with the name of a planet). "My Very Excellent Mother Just Sat Upon Nine Pins" (Mercury, Venus, Earth, Mars, Jupiter, Saturn, Uranus, Neptune, and Pluto).

_____ **Use "Rap":** Recite the terms, or words you are trying to memorize with a rap rhythm. This beat can help you memorize much faster.

Taking a Test*

_____ **Prepare:** Make sure you have enough time to study for the test. Sometimes it may help to have a study partner or team. Also, make sure you get enough rest and have a healthy breakfast before the test.

_____ **Reduce Stress:** Think of the test as a challenge. If you are worried, slow down. Take a few slow, deep breaths and make positive statements to yourself about how you are capable of succeeding on the test.

_____ **Become Motivated:** Remember that each test is important and don't quit trying. Give each question your best effort.

_____ **Be Test-Wise:** Know how to make a good guess and be careful not to go too slow or too fast.

Studying Effectively at Home

_____ **Manage Your Time:** Use your time wisely. Set a time to start working and stick with it, without having to be reminded by your parents.

_____ **Prevent Distractions:** You will accomplish more in less time if you do not have a television or phone nearby. Find a place to study that is private and comfortable. Some students find that soft music can help them block out distractions and concentrate better.

Using Resource People

_____ **Ask Your Teacher:** Don't be afraid to ask your teacher for assistance. It shows you care.

_____ **Ask Other School Resource Staff:** There are several people in your school who may help you if you ask.

_____ **Ask Other Students:** Other students may be very willing to help you or work with you. Perhaps you can form a study group.

_____ **Ask Your Family:** Don't forget that others in your family can be great resources.

_____ **Ask Other People:** There may be other people in your community who would be pleased to help you. Some communities have tutoring and other student assistance programs available.

* Adapted from **The Test Buster Pep Rally** by R. P. Bowman (Educational Media, 1987).

Follow-Up:
First look over all items that your Pilot rated a "4" or "5" and recognize his/her strong points. Then look at the items your Pilot rated a "1" or "2." Help him/her set goals to improve in these areas. Then assist your Pilot in selecting an area you will begin working on together.

Other Activities

Activity 52 *(Grades 2-5):* If your Pilot is old enough to be receiving homework assignments from school, help him/her make a "Schoolwork Survival Kit." Decorate a small box and fill it with items like scissors, pencils, pens, crayons, etc. Perhaps attach or insert a "Homework Plan" consisting of a commitment to the place(s) and times studying will take place.

Activity 53 *(Grades 2-5):* Form a "Parent Partnership." Work with your Pilot's parent(s)/guardian(s) to help him/her develop or improve study habits at home. You can become a valuable reinforcer to your Pilot when parents give you a positive report of his/her special accomplishments. You might develop a "Homework Coupon" to give to your Pilot. After your Pilot earns five coupons, you might take him/her for breakfast or give a small token gift.

Activity 54 *(Grades 2-5):* Help your Pilot find a "study buddy" who can work with him/her on schoolwork. The two students could meet after school at each other's home or talk on the telephone about schoolwork. The school guidance counselor may be able to help you find someone.

LESSON 8: "MY UNDERSTANDING OF ALCOHOL"

We should be teaching children as early as possible about the risks of drinking alcohol. Children should be made aware that some elementary school students try drinking alcohol and that this is wrong and dangerous.

There are many reasons why young people begin to drink alcohol. Helping children to explore these reasons will help them watch for situations in which they will say "No!" without hesitation. Children will also benefit by learning a collection of clear reasons for not drinking alcohol.

Activity 55: Why Some Kids Start Drinking Alcohol

Grades 3-5
Materials: One copy of the following checklist.

The following are excuses some young people give to explain why they started drinking alcohol. Although there are no good reasons for kids to drink look through these excuses with your Pilot and check the ones that you both believe are the most common.

☐ They want to have fun.

☐ They want to feel accepted by others.

☐ They want to live dangerously.

☐ It helps them to relax.

☐ They want to forget their problems.

☐ They think it helps them socialize.

☐ There's nothing else they can think of to do.

☐ They like how it tastes.

☐ It quenches their thirst.

☐ They are curious about what will happen.

☐ Their parents drink.

☐ Their friends drink.

☐ They are trying to act like they are older.

☐ Because of commercials about alcohol.

☐ They think it will make them "cool."

☐ They are rebelling against their parents.

☐ They want to attract the opposite sex.

☐ It is inherited from their parents.

Activity 56: Reasons for Not Drinking Alcohol

Grades 3-5
Materials: One copy of the following checklist.

The following are some of the reasons why kids should not drink alcohol. Check the ones that you both believe are the best reasons.

- ☐ It can make you throw up.
- ☐ You may end up doing things that you regret.
- ☐ It is illegal and you may get caught.
- ☐ It can cause you problems at school and at home.
- ☐ It can result in a terrible hangover.
- ☐ It can keep you from having fun in other ways.
- ☐ Drinking too much alcohol can kill you
- ☐ It can make you even more angry or very sad.
- ☐ It can cause you to not care about yourself.
- ☐ You can end up in a dangerous situation.
- ☐ It is addictive and can be hard to quit.
- ☐ Sooner or later, it can kill you.
- ☐ It can hurt your relationships with people in your family.
- ☐ You can lose respect from others your age.
- ☐ You can be taken advantage of in different ways.
- ☐ It can make you lazy.
- ☐ When you have a job, it can cause you to be fired.
- ☐ It makes you somebody that you are not.

Other Activities

Activity 57 *(Grades 2-5):* With your Pilot, make up a skit about the negative effects of drinking alcohol. Ask a teacher if you can present your skit to their class. For example, a skit could be made showing someone falling down, becoming sick, getting into a car accident, or not being able to talk clearly. Or, develop a skit titled, "This is Your (body part) on Alcohol." Affected body parts include brain, liver, stomach, kidneys, eyes, legs, etc. Demonstrate with a prop, or with body movements, the body part affected by alcohol. You might check with the school media specialist, health professional, and/or counselor for information and materials on this topic that are appropriate for the age of the children.

Activity 58 *(Grades 2-5):* Look through magazines and/or newspapers for advertisements of alcoholic beverages. Try to determine the strategy the advertiser is using to try to show that drinking alcohol is "cool." Cut out several of these ads and make a collage together. Talk about how these ads encourage kids to want to drink.

Activity 59 *(Grades 2-5):* Look for a story or book on teen or pre-teen drinking. Consult your local library or school media center. Read through one of the stories or books together with your Pilot. Stop several times during your reading of the story to discuss the situations being described.

LESSON 9: "MY UNDERSTANDING OF OTHER DRUGS"

Overall, drug abuse in youths aged 12-17 has risen by almost 80% between 1992 and 1995 according to a federal government survey.* This alarming trend indicates that new and fresh approaches are needed to discourage the use of intoxicants **before** children's first drug experience.

There are several programs available that help children learn about the dangers of drugs. Most of them present information to children in classes, books, and assembly programs. The Co-Pilot program provides a more personalized opportunity for a child to receive and discuss this kind of information about drugs within the context of a one-to-one relationship with a mentor. The following activities will provide opportunities to discuss illegal drugs, alternatives to their use, and different ways to say "No!"

*Newsweek, August 26, 1996, p. 52.

Activity 60: Who Would You Go To For Help?

Grades K-5

Materials: One copy of the following situations and list of helpers.

Read one the following situations to your Pilot and ask, "Who would you go to for help?" Then read through the list of helpers and allow your Pilot to select any that he/she might go to for help in that situation. Discuss others on the list that your Pilot could also seek help from.

1. An older student shows you some pills and asks you to take one of them.

2. Some students your age start pressuring you to sniff gasoline.

3. Someone tries to get you to drink some beer.

4. Someone in your family has a drug problem.

5. A friend of yours tries to get you to smoke a cigarette.

Helpers:

- Teacher
- Parents
- Principal
- Police (DARE Officer)
- Counselor
- Nurse
- Other students
- Other Person

Activity 61: "I've Heard of It"

Grades 3-5

Materials: One copy of the following checklist.

Ask your Pilot to look over the following list and place one of the following symbols in the space before each item to indicate how familiar he/she is with the substance. Help your Pilot learn where he/she can get more information about the dangers of any of these substances.

X = "I know a lot about it."
O = "I know a little about it."
? = "I'm not sure what this is."

☐ Marijuana

☐ Alcohol

☐ Caffeine

☐ Tobacco

☐ LSD

☐ Cocaine or Crack

☐ Angel Dust (PCP)

☐ Ecstasy

☐ Heroin

☐ 'Shrooms (psychedelic mushrooms)

☐ Speed (crystal meth)

☐ Downers (barbiturates or tranquilizers)

☐ Steroids (for body building)

☐ Inhalants (like gasoline or glue)

☐ Others (list)

_____

_____

_____

_____

Activity 62: Fun Without Drugs

Grades 3-5
Materials: One copy of the following checklist.

Some adults believe that the main reason that kids begin using drugs is because someone pushes them into it. However, the fact is that the primary reasons kids give for using alcohol, or other drugs is because they want to have fun. They decide to try drugs without actually being pushed.

For young people to make the decision to never use drugs, it is important for them to have many things they can do to have fun without being intoxicated or high. Ask your Pilot to place a check mark in the front of each of the following things he/she would like to do to have fun without drugs.

☐ Play team sports such as baseball, basketball, soccer, football, or hockey.

☐ Play any of the above sports, without being on a formal team.

☐ Play games such as pool, chess, checkers, cards, video games, or board games.

☐ Go bowling with some friends.

☐ Go skating or skateboarding with friends.

☐ Go snow skiing or sledding with friends.

☐ Go swimming or boating with friends.

☐ Learn to play a musical instrument.

☐ Listen to music alone or with friends.

☐ Write poetry, music, and/or lyrics.

☐ Create something with arts or crafts.

☐ Get involved in one or more interest clubs.

☐ Take up a hobby such as collecting something.

☐ Take up martial arts.

☐ Hang out only with friends who are drug free.

☐ Go to the shopping mall.

☐ Go camping or hiking.

☐ Plan a trip with your friends.

☐ Go biking.

☐ Go to a local recreational facility.

☐ Watch television.

☐ Go to the movies.

☐ Learn to cook something special.

☐ Go to watch a sports team practice or play.

☐ Go to a park with some friends.

☐ Make up your own dance routine.

☐ Visit your local humane society and help care for the animals.

☐ Try out for a part in a play.

☐ Join a community youth group.

☐ Invent a game to play by yourself or with friends.

☐ Organize a neighborhood carnival.

☐ Build something with your friends.

☐ Go fishing.

Activity 63: A Message to a Child

Grades 3-5
Materials: None

Ask your Pilot, "If you were going to talk with a first grader about drugs, what are three things you would say?" Have your Pilot write his/her answers below. Then discuss them together.

1. _____

_____

_____

2. _____

_____

_____

3. _____

_____

_____

Other Activities

Activity 64 *(Grades K-5):* Brainstorm a list of different ways to say "No!" to someone who might offer a student a chance to use drugs. Help your Pilot practice saying these things by role-playing different situations together.

Examples of statements include:

"No way!"   **"I've got to go!"**

"Get away from me!"   **"Never!"**

"I said 'No' and I mean 'No'!"

"Forget it!"

Activity 65 *(Grades 3-5):* Set up a time for you and your Pilot to interview a social worker, health care worker, or the school's DARE Officer about drug problems in your community. Before the interview, decide together what questions each of you will ask.

Or, arrange to visit and interview a drug rehabilitation counselor with your Pilot. Ask if you can have some brochures and other available information on drugs. Then, work with your Pilot to create a presentation for younger students in the school. Note that there are several other sources for this information in your community. Check with your Pilot's school counselor for ideas on who to contact.

Activity 66 *(Grades 3-5):* Work with your Pilot and perhaps with others in your program to organize a drug-free event in your school or community.

LESSON 10: "MY CHARACTER"

Being successful means more than merely having money, power, and other things that show your accomplishments. These things are merely signs that you have achieved some things. They do not show what kind of person you are on the inside. Character building is one way to work on your inner self. It focuses on things about you that are eventually going to be much more important in determining your success and happiness than mere symbols of success.

Parents, teachers, and anyone else who is attempting to help a child to grow, should work together to help him/her realize the importance of the following "Six Pillars of Character."

1. Trustworthiness

2. Respect

3. Responsibility

4. Fairness

5. Caring

6. Citizenship

Activity 67: Learn "The Six Pillars of Character"

Grades K-5
Materials: One copy of the "The Six Pillars of Character."

Discuss with your Pilot one of the Six Pillars of Character. Talk together about what each word means and why it is important. You might find the following list helpful in providing examples of each Pillar. Afterwards, do something together with your Pilot to show this type of character. Whenever you notice your Pilot showing one of these Pillars, be sure to mention it to him/her.

The Six Pillars of Character*

1. Trustworthiness
- Be honest.
- If you find something that doesn't belong to you, return it to the owner.
- Don't cheat or steal other people's property.

2. Respect
- Be courteous and polite with others.
- Don't put other people down.
- Accept other people's differences.

3. Responsibility
- Keep your promises.
- Be reliable.
- Set a good example of behavior for others.

4. Fairness
- Be a good listener of other people's views.
- Don't take advantage of others.
- Take only your fair share.

5. Caring
- Show kindness toward others.
- Live by the Golden Rule—treat others the way you want them to treat you.
- Don't be selfish, mean, or cruel to others.

6. Citizenship
- Obey school rules.
- Obey the law.
- Be helpful to others.

*Reprinted from *Ethics: Easier Said Than Done* with permission of the Josephson Institute of Ethics ©1992

Activity 68: Trustworthiness

Grades 3-5
Materials: None

For each of the following situations, ask your Pilot, "What did the person(s) do that was wrong?" "What could have been done differently to show better character?" "What could the person(s) do next to work things out?"

- ☞ Ron saw another student drop a dollar bill on the floor. He picked up the money and put it in his pocket. Later, Ron spent it on some candy.

- ☞ Mara told a secret to her friend about a boy that she liked. Later that afternoon, Mara found out that several other students found out about it, and they started teasing her.

- ☞ Todd was worried about taking a test. He knew that the student sitting next to him would probably do well on it. During the test, Todd looked at the student's paper and copied some of the answers.

Activity 69: Respect

Grades 3-5
Materials: None

Continue the same procedures with the following:

- ☞ A group of students were making fun of a girl because of the way she looked. John heard the other students tease her, and then started making fun of the girl too.

- ☞ Several students were going to Natalie's birthday party. But one girl said she couldn't come because of her religion. Natalie became angry and said to the other girls, "That's just an excuse! She just doesn't want to come."

- ☞ The teacher told Matt to stop talking with others and get to work. Matt kept on talking, anyway.

Activity 70: Responsibility

Grades 3-5
Materials: None

Continue the same procedures with the following:

☞ John promised his parents that he would go straight home and clean up his room after school. Instead, he went to the park with his friends.

☞ LaToya didn't complete any of her homework for the third day in a row. She told her teacher that she forgot it again.

☞ Brian borrowed a CD from a friend. While he had it, Brian lent it to another friend who lost it.

Activity 71: Fairness

Grades 3-5
Materials: None

Continue the same procedures with the following:

☞ Michael heard from other students that Jeremy stole his lunch money out of his desk. When Jeremy wasn't around, Michael reached into Jeremy's desk and took something of his.

☞ Two girls worked equally hard on a science project. Once they finished, one girl told the teacher that she had done most of the work.

☞ Darla used to be best friends with Patricia. Then Patricia started spending time with another girl. So, Darla made up a lie about the other girl and told it to several people.

Activity 72: Caring

Grades 3-5
Materials: None

Continue the same procedures with the following:

☞ A new boy in school began to cry as he sat at his desk. Some of the other students started laughing at him.

☞ Krista tried to tell Carrie that she was sorry for something she did. Carrie just looked away and kept walking without saying a word.

☞ During the winter, Carla's parents told her that they were having money problems and asked her to please keep the front door to the house closed better so that the heat wouldn't be wasted. That evening, Carla locked her bedroom door, put on her coat, and opened up her window. Then she lit up a cigarette and blew the smoke out the window.

Activity 73: Citizenship

Grades K-5
Materials: None

Continue the same procedures with the following:

☞ Jason heard that one of his friends was going to steal money from the teacher's desk. He didn't want to say anything because he didn't want to lose his friend.

☞ Mark stole a computer game from a large store. He said that the store was owned by rich people who have "plenty of money."

☞ Barbara never volunteered to help anyone unless she received something for it.

Other Activities

Activity 74 *(Grades K-5):* Have a "Character Scavenger Hunt" with the other Pilots and Co-Pilots. Each Pilot/Co-Pilot pair should hunt for examples of people showing each of the Six Pillars. These examples may be found by observing students at play during recess or at lunch. They may also be found in magazine pictures, books, or on television.

Activity 75 *(Grades K-5):* Have your Pilot draw or construct six large pillars holding up a paper or cardboard roof. On each pillar should be labeled the name of the character trait. Then, use this as a backdrop for mini-plays about each Pillar of Character. Have your Pilot use small figures of people and/or animals to act out the stories.

LESSON 11:
"My Future Career"

Your career may seem like a long way off in the future. But, now is the time to begin thinking about different careers that are interesting to you.

There are many different kinds of jobs that you could do when you grow up. Some of these jobs involve working with a team of people. Other jobs involve working with machines and equipment. Some jobs include working outdoors. Other jobs take place in an office. Some jobs involve taking care of animals or people. Other jobs involve showing your art, music, or sports talents. There are many, many kinds of jobs to choose from.

Activity 76: Career Charades
Grades K-5
Materials: 10-20 index cards

Write the name of a different career on each of 10-20 index cards. Then place these cards in a bag or box and shake them up. Next, you and your Pilot each take a turn picking out a card and acting out the career while the other tries to guess what it is. Afterwards, take some time to discuss your Pilot's understanding of and feelings toward the career.

Activity 77: Service Learning
Grades K-5
Materials: None

Find a service learning project in your community which you and your Pilot can complete together. Service learning involves students in field projects that attempt to meet some community need. Examples of service learning projects include:

- Adopting a grandparent at a nursing home.
- Planting a tree, bush, or flower.
- Helping to keep an area of a park clean.
- Making a gift to send to a needy person in your community.
- Putting together a "care package" for a child from another country.
- Adopting a friend at a local children's home.
- Volunteering to care for animals at a local wildlife shelter.

When working together on a service learning project, help your Pilot explore how the experience is good preparation for working in a career. For example, it may help him/her to learn how to be more generous, dependable, hard working, persistent, and/or committed.

Activity 78: Family Career Tree
Grades K-5
Materials: Large sheet of drawing paper or poster board, index cards, crayons or magic markers, tape or paste.

Have your Pilot draw and/or write about the careers of different family members. If possible ask your Pilot to interview family members and describe each on an index card. Other cards could be completed on ancestors.

Then, ask your Pilot to draw a tree on a large sheet of drawing paper or poster board. Then, tape or paste each index card onto the tree. Your Pilot may create his/her tree following a "Family Tree" format. Or, your Pilot could merely draw a tree and place the cards randomly in the branches.

Activity 79: Job Shadowing
Grades K-5
Materials: None

Arrange for your Pilot to visit you at your work setting. Allow him/her to observe you at work and become involved in a job related task, if this is possible and appropriate. In addition, you might arrange for your Pilot to shadow workers in other careers. Or, you might work out a time for your Pilot to meet and shadow a high school student who is currently taking classes in a vocational program.

Activity 80: Career Field Trips
Grades K-5
Materials: None

Arrange field trips for your Pilot to visit different career settings where he/she can observe people at work. For example, visit a hospital, factory, farm, police or fire department, local government office, department store, airport, or construction project.

Activity 81: Tools of the Trade
Grades K-5
Materials: Drawing paper (4-10 sheets), crayons or magic markers

Ask your Pilot to make a booklet filled with drawings of tools used in different careers. Each page will display the name of the career and the tools used. As an option, help your Pilot collect some real tools and make a display for other children to learn about the careers.

Activity 82: What's Important to You?

Grades 3-5
Materials: A copy of the following list.

The following are some of the reasons why people choose and enjoy certain careers over others. Ask your Pilot to select the three most important things he/she would like to find in a career. Then, have your Pilot rank these three items according to what is most important to him/her. Follow-up with a discussion about what careers might be most suited to your Pilot.

- ☐ Working with others in a team
- ☐ Working alone
- ☐ Working outdoors
- ☐ Being my own boss
- ☐ Fixing or repairing things
- ☐ Working with computers
- ☐ Working with people or animals
- ☐ Working with numbers
- ☐ Playing a sport
- ☐ Entertaining others
- ☐ Drawing or painting
- ☐ Traveling
- ☐ Selling things
- ☐ Helping people solve their problems
- ☐ Playing a musical instrument or singing
- ☐ Building things

Other Activities

Activity 83 *(Grades K-5)*: Ask your Pilot to interview different adults at his/her school and at home. Your Pilot should ask the adults what careers they thought about when they were in elementary school. Then, what different jobs did they have before they entered the career they are in presently. Discuss with your Pilot how some people change careers several times during their lives.

Activity 84 *(Grades K-5)*: In your community, find someone (not related to your Pilot) who will pay a minimal fee to you and your Pilot for completing some brief job. Then, go with your Pilot to interview for the job. Next, schedule a time to do the job and emphasize the importance of getting there ready and on time. Then, work together to complete the task and share the pay between you. It is important to not give your Pilot all the money. Emphasize how you worked as partners. For example, rake or clean a yard, mop a floor, sweep a porch or sidewalk, or cook a special meal for someone.

Activity 85 *(Grades K-5)*: Go to the local library with your Pilot. Together, look up books on three to five careers that interest him/her. Explore some of these books together and discuss how these careers are similar and how they are different from one another.

THREE CO-PILOTING STORIES

1. Martha's Story

(Martha is an elementary school teacher.)

The first day the school staff reported back to school last year, I already felt overwhelmed with all the work I anticipated that I needed to complete before the students arrived the next week. I couldn't have imagined volunteering to become involved in something "extra." But, Mr. Jackson made such an inspirational presentation about a mentoring program that I couldn't resist. I volunteered to become a mentor and it was one of the most rewarding programs I have ever become involved in.

Our principal allowed those of us who volunteered for the program to use one of our in-service days to meet for the mentor training. The 14 people in our group worked through the Co-Piloting Mentor training program together. Some of us were more comfortable doing activities than others, but all of us participated and found the training to be very interesting and useful. We discussed and practiced mentoring strategies and networked with each other on ideas for mentoring disadvantaged children. We also received mentor handbooks full of ideas and activities to use with our "Pilots." I eagerly awaited the next week when I would begin working with my Pilot, Kenya.

Kenya was a second grader who had low self-esteem. We were told we needed to meet with the children at least once each week. But after awhile, Kenya and I started meeting three times per week; once during my Monday planning period, again after school on Wednesday, and then during lunch on Friday. In addition, occasionally I found times that I could walk down the hallway to say "hello" to her and talk briefly.

Later, I made a visit to Kenya's home and met her mother. She was very appreciative of my work with her daughter. She gave me several insights that helped me identify abilities in Kenya that I wasn't aware of.

By the end of the year, Kenya and I had grown very close and both of us decided to continue meeting with one another. Over the summer, I called her on the phone a few times to see how she was doing. I also sent her a birthday card with a little gift.

This year, Kenya and I have spent more time working through several of the "Self-Improvement Activities." Also, Kenya and I have been compiling her "Pilot Portfolio" consisting of samples of her school work and products of our work together.

But, last fall, Kenya began to have more difficulties with her schoolwork, so I helped her mother arrange for a tutor. I also tried to provide Kenya with even more encouragement and support. Later, when she learned that she would be promoted to fourth grade, Kenya and I had a private celebration.

We both plan to continue meeting as Pilot and Co-Pilot next year which will make three years of working together. After that, if all continues to go well with her schoolwork, Kenya will be leaving our school. That will be a sad occasion for both of us. Being a mentor/Co-Pilot with Kenya has been one of the most personally and professionally rewarding experiences of my career as a professional educator.

2. William's Story

(William is an employee of a large corporation.)

I work for a large insurance company. Last year, our Employee Assistance Director made a presentation about a Co-Piloting program that he was organizing. Our company has conducted several initiatives to "give back to the community" but this mentoring program especially caught my attention. The Co-Piloting program was well thought out and organized, and seemed to be something that might make a great difference in the lives of some disadvantaged youth. Prior to being matched with a child, we had to attend two evening sessions. Then we would become official "Co-Pilots."

After we completed training, we began making weekly half-hour visits to the school to meet with our Pilots who were kindergartners and first graders. At first, we became "Lunch Buddies" to our little friends and ate with them each Friday. Later, we also began to meet with them in the school media center, where there were several books and other resources available. Our Pilots were asked to choose a book for us to read with them at the beginning of each meeting. Then, we picked activities and projects from our Co-Piloting handbooks to use with our little Pilots.

By the way, the title of this program, "Co-Piloting" caught my attention partly because one of my pastimes is flying an airplane. The last time I flew to the city airport, I asked for some plastic pilot pins (wings) at one of the airline gates. They were pleased to donate them for our little "Pilots." Each time we began working with the children, we would pin on the little wing insignias. When we completed the program, we gave the children the wings to keep.

My Pilot's name is David. At first, he seemed like a quiet, shy little fellow. Then, as I gave him more attention, he seemed to warm up to me more quickly. Later, to my surprise, there were a few times when David became overly excited and the Program Coordinator helped me to calm him down. David loved being a Pilot. So, for a special surprise I asked his parents if I could take him for a ride in my plane. David had not even been on an elevator before, and he had never been close to a real airplane. His parents gave me permission, and we have flown three times together now. During our flights, I gave David some things to do such as look for the runway as we made our landing approach. He loved it! Now, David tells me that he wants to be a professional pilot someday.

After 18 weeks, the program was over. David and I said our good-byes, but I still call him now and then. Becoming a Co-Pilot in a little person's life is a very rewarding experience for the child and for the adult who works with him/her. Though I realize there are a lot of mentoring programs for disadvantaged adolescents, I think I'm partial to a Co-Pilot program which involves us with children. After all, the earlier we start working with some of these kids, the better.

3. Shane's Story

(Shane is a sophomore in college, hoping to graduate one day with a teaching certificate.)

I have always liked helping kids. I have two little brothers at home and so I know how to relate with younger people. The Co-Piloting program helped me learn a lot of new things that will help me mentor a young person.

At our college, we are required to provide service to our community. We went to a one-day training retreat led by the Coordinator of our Co-Pilot program. Thirty-eight students volunteered to become mentors in the program.

After training, I went to the elementary school where I met "Noodles," a fifth grade boy. He told me he got that name from other kids because of his hair, which was in dreads. He said he liked the nickname and wanted me to use it with him, so I did.

When Noodles first met me he didn't say very much, so I tried asking him the best questions I could. However, the more questions I asked him the less he seemed to talk. Then I remembered from my Co-Pilot training that we weren't supposed to ask too many questions. So, I took him to the basketball court and we shot baskets together. This is what finally loosened him up toward me. After about four weeks Noodles began telling me about some of his feelings about things. I think he had a low self-concept and needed someone like me to listen to him and support him.

I guess the best thing I did for Noodles was to be there for him. He loved it when I just sat back and listened to him tell me anything that was on his mind. Sometimes it seemed like the less I said, the more he talked. He told me he was very unhappy at home, and that he felt that no one really thought that he would amount to anything in his life. He and I worked through some of the Co-Pilot Self-Improvement Activities. They helped us talk even more about what he could do to improve himself. I never really gave him much advice. I mainly listened to him talk, and encouraged him whenever I could. We also spent a lot of time doing projects. Together, wedeveloped a lesson for kids in elementary school called "Tobacco Facts." We presented it to two first grade classes and the kids really liked it. Noodles was very proud to have the children admire our presentation.

During our final meeting, Noodles and I went out for pizza. I was shocked when I noticed for the first time, that he was wearing a button down dress shirt. He said that he bought it the previous weekend. The shirt looked very similar to the ones I had been wearing whenever I met with him. I never mentioned it to him, but I think Noodles was trying to imitate me a little. I believe that Noodles benefited in many ways as a result of our Co-Pilot program. I, too, learned much about how to connect with an at-risk young person and help him become motivated to do more positive things for himself.

References

Bowman, R.P. (1987). *The Test Buster Pep Rally*. Minneapolis, MN: Educational Media.

Bowman, R.P. (1997). *Study With a Buddy*. Chapin, SC: YouthLight, Inc. (In development).

Bowman, R.P. & Chanaca, J. Jr. (1993) *Peer Pals*. Circle Pines, MN: American Guidance Services.

Josephson Institute of Ethics (Dec., 1992). *Developing Moral Values in Youth. Ethics: Easier Said Than Done.* (Marina Del Rey, CA), Issues 19&20, 80-81.

Klots, S. (1995). *Carl Lewis Story*. New York: Chelsea House Publishers

Mosley, L.(1976). *Charles Lindbergh*. Garden City, New York: Doubleday.

Rich, D.L. (1993). *Queen Bess: Daredevil Aviator*. Washington, D.C.: Smithsonian Institute Press.